ETHNICITY, PLURALISM, AND RACE

ETHNICITY, PLURALISM, AND RACE

Race Relations Theory in America Before Myrdal

R. FRED WACKER

Contributions in Sociology, Number 42

GREENWOOD PRESS
WESTPORT, CONNECTICUT
LONDON, ENGLAND

HT
1521
, W25
1983

Library of Congress Cataloging in Publication Data

Wacker, R. Fred.
  Ethnicity, pluralism, and race.

  (Contributions in sociology, ISSN 0084-9278 ; no. 42)
  Bibliography: p.
  Includes index.
  1. Race relations—Philosophy. 2. Ethnicity—
Philosophy. 3. Pluralism (Social sciences) 4. Chicago
school of sociology. 5. Sociology—United States—
Methodology. I. Title. II. Series.
HT1521.W25 1983   305.8'001   82-11687
ISBN 0-313-23580-5 (lib. bdg.)

Library of Congress Catalog Card Number: 82-11687
ISBN: 0-313-23580-5
ISSN: 0084-9278

First published in 1983

Greenwood Press
A division of Congressional Information Service, Inc.
88 Post Road West
Westport, Connecticut 06881

Printed in the United States of America

10 9 8 7 6 5 4 3 2 1

CONTENTS

ACKNOWLEDGMENTS

I would like to thank the following scholars for their help and criticism while this work was underway: Robert Sklar, Frank Rossiter, Bazel Allen, Edward Tiryakian, John Higham, and the late Klaus Reigel. Persons associated with the Chicago dynamic who were kind and granted me some insight into that social and intellectual atmosphere include Herbert Blumer, Everett Hughes, Edgar Thompson, Guy Johnson, David Reisman, Andrew Greeley, the late Dorothy Thomas, Edward Shils, Robert E. L. Faris, and especially Morris Janowitz. Rolland Wright, Gordon Hinzmann, Marc Cogan, Robert K. Thomas and Merrill Jackson are Wayne State faculty who were truly collegial. Finally, thanks go to my family, especially Sally, John, Margaret, and Ruth and to the scholar's extended families, the staffs at the libraries at Chicago, Fisk, Michigan, and Wayne State and the Library of Congress.

INTRODUCTION

The following study had its origins in the contentious years of the late 1960s and the early 1970s. During those years the constituent disciplines of the social sciences and humanities were attacked from several different perspectives. If the criticisms had a common theme, however, it was that previous generations of scholars had failed to develop an adequate and comprehensive picture of American social reality. The social and cultural conflicts of the 1960s—racial, ethnic, and intergenerational—highlighted the diverse and often divisive nature of American society. One significant intellectual consequence of those conflicts was the emergent criticism of the social thought and social science of the past as too complacent and too committed to a consensus bias or ideology.

During these years, and continuing up to the present, moreover, new cohorts became active within American universities and within the social science disciplines (but especially within those fields with a traditionally humanistic base—sociology, anthropology, history, and psychology). Blacks and ethnics (and later women) who entered the university systems were sensitized not only to the pervasiveness of conflict within American society but also to the increased racial and ethnic consciousness (and later women's group consciousness) which marked that decade and its general and academic politics. From these groups a series of criticisms emerged which threatened the various establishments within disciplines and particular institutions.

In retrospect it is clear that the revitalization of group identity and assertiveness since the 1960s has had a significant impact upon the liberal intellectual and scholarly community in America. Since the vast majority of that broad community were committed to and identified with a belief in the ideal of the integration of all "minority groups" in America and especially of black Americans, that impact was inevitable. The development of more particularistic identities among blacks and other groups threatened and placed under great strain the compound of secular, universalist, and cosmopolitan values which nearly all intellectuals and scholars had imbibed and introjected as part of their socialization into that community.[1]

I do not wish to overemphasize the particular force of these movements of group consciousness upon the established communities. Undoubtedly the collective impact of those movements upon liberal communities and thought patterns was confounded with the strains imposed by other fractious issues such as the debate over the conduct of war in Southeast Asia and the rise of student protest and violence. Yet, even after the Vietnamese War had ground to its numbing conclusion and the campuses had become more tranquil, the issues raised by racial, ethnic, and sexual identity and demands remained a potent source of contention. It is most probable, in fact, that the continued commitment to affirmative action programs and an emphasis on entitlements within a welfare state context will provide a continuing impetus toward racial and ethnic identification and demands.[2]

The criticisms of American social thought and social science, then, should be seen as part of a much wider and pervasive political, cultural, and institutional upheaval. In this study I will be primarily concerned with criticisms of the discipline most implicated in the study of race and ethnicity, sociology, although a similar study could be made of the criticisms of anthropology or history or other humanistic or cultural disciplines. My broader aim is to correct the distortions and misinterpretations of its past history. According to the portrayals of common in the years around 1970, the liberalism of American sociologists in general and most experts in race and ethnicity in particular was deficient. It was hardly possible for young "militants" and revisionists to claim that sociology had ignored the study of racial and ethnic groups, since of all the social sciences and humanities, sociology had been the most constant in its attention to the group basis of American life. The attacks had to center upon the "ideology" of sociology.

The criticisms which began around the mid-1960s first centered upon the work and the policy implications of such contemporary social scientists as Daniel P. Moynihan, Edward Banfield, and Oscar Lewis. They were criticized for portraying black Americans and other minority groups as locked into a culture of poverty. Their emphasis upon the psychological and family-centered determinants of poverty, it was argued, ignored important racist, class, and political causes of impoverishment. They were chastised for an inadequate vision of culture, since they failed to recognize forms of cultural persistence and strength within racial and ethnic groups. The general implication of their work, an implication with vital consequences for public policy, was that pervasive racism and structural inequalities were less important than pathologies within minority groups and families and that most minority cultures were inferior to middle-class, white culture.[3]

The patterns of thought established during the 1960s in the criticism of social scientists like Moynihan, Banfield, and Lewis were central to the emerging critical consciousness of many scholars. As they looked into their collective past, into the history of their disciplines, they made use of the tools fashioned in the critique of contemporary social science. Most important for our purposes, the roots of the culture of poverty "ideology" were found in the assimilationist and even racist theoretical and empirical work of earlier social scientists. The so-called assimilationist ideology was largely traced to the Chicago "school" of sociology and social science.[4]

It was the Chicago cluster of social scientists that was the dominant group of scholars dealing with race and ethnicity in the formative period of modern American sociology.[5] The theoretical and empirical work of the professors at Chicago—W. I. Thomas and Robert E. Park—and that of their prominent students such as Louis Wirth, Charles S. Johnson, E. Franklin Frazier, E. C. Hughes, was the most prestigious and exemplary in American sociology at least up to the 1950s. The criticisms of the 1960s and 1970s, however, sought to disqualify most of the work of these men as objective social science and thus cut out the heart of a long tradition of scholarship in the area of race and ethnicity.

There were two damaging criticisms of Chicago sociology in this area. First, the Chicago cluster was portrayed as formulating a rigid idea that all ethnic and racial groups would pass through a race relations cycle and end up assimilated to white Anglo-Saxon values.[6] Second, the Chicago perspective, it was argued, paid little attention to the persistence of minority cultures, since they were assumed to be gradually disappearing. A part of this neglect was the general inability to recognize that black Americans possessed a distinctive culture.[7]

These charges and the works in which they appeared are not without any foundation, but they do not carry the weight their proponents attributed to them. In comparison with the vast bulk of American social scientists, not to mention less liberal elements in American intellectual life, the Chicago group had a differentiated and sophisticated view of racial and ethnic groups in America. In the work of a few key Chicago sociologists such as Robert Park, E. Franklin Frazier, and E. C. Hughes the analysis of American groups was only a component part of a worldwide comparative vision of social processes. Although the closer analysis of the empirical work of the Chicago cluster will be taken up below, it is significant that critics cannot point to any empirical work which was guided by the race relations cycle idea. The second major criticism, that Chicago sociology was insensitive to ethnic persistence, is obviously connected to the first, since if the ultimate stage is assimilation there will be little if anything to study once the logic of the race relations cycle works itself out. Yet even here, where it is clear from the record of Chicago scholarship that little work was done on failures of assimilation or cultural resistance or persistence, the lack of attention of the social scientists needs to be analyzed more deeply.

The most exemplary work of the early Chicago research tradition—W. I. Thomas's and Florian Znaniecki's *The Polish Peasant*—had as one of its central themes the persistence of the meanings and attitudes among the Polish immigrants. In fact, it was this theme of Thomas's which formed much of the theory of Robert Park in the 1920s as Park achieved a central theoretical status at Chicago after Thomas left in 1919.[8] Park was most cognizant of the weight of tradition and culture within some groups, especially American blacks and others from what were termed "folk" backgrounds; yet his prominent students apparently turned away from this aspect of the Thomas-Park heritage. This neglect and its implications deserves further analysis and will be dealt with below.

The Chicago cluster of scholars and the concepts, theories, and exemplary works they perpetuated, then, were portrayed as impediments to the full development of an adequate analysis of American group life. The present-minded and often shallow manner in which this portion of the heritage of sociology was dealt with, however, was linked to another set of themes in the critique of sociology's past. This strain of criticism bypassed the Chicago school of the 1920s and 1930s to peer into the darker racist past of American social science. The works of several "founding fathers" of social science—E. A. Ross, W. I. Thomas, Howard Odum, and others—were attacked for their racialist and hereditarian assumptions and conclusions. The revisionist scholars of the 1960s discovered that many of the founders' works, all written prior to 1920 we should note, were marked by an emphasis upon the racial characteristics or "temperaments" of immigrant or racial groups. The term "race" was used with abandon and the conceptual framework of these early scholars was criticized as racist. This early scholars was criticized as racist. This early racism was often seen as infecting American social science as a whole.[9]

Most of these attacks upon the racist roots of American social science were made, of course, in a polemical atmosphere and often were part of a strategy of guilt by association. But it is also true that there were few substantial histories of the early years of American social science and fewer analyses of the intellectual framework of these "Progressive Era" scholars. This situation has been remedied to some extent and the early decades of this century should not be ignored in any larger reinterpretation of the ideology and biases of American sociology.

It is worth noting here that these two general groups of social scientists—the Chicago cluster and the founding fathers—have been criticized, often by the same people, for committing opposite sins. Whereas the hereditarians believed that blacks and many European, Asian, and Latin American immigrants were morally, physically, or intellectually inferior to old, "native," and white Anglo-Saxon groups, the assimilationist tended to believe that blacks and immigrants were different in only minor ways. Yet in the polemical atmosphere of the period around 1970, and in more isolated instances up through the next decade, the assimilationists were often attacked as being as "racist" or culturally arrogant as the founding fathers. The assimilationists, it was repeatedly claimed, thought that all groups would shed their distinctive cultures and become WASPS. Often this latter charge was linked to a further assumption that if only social scientists had not been so confident in the automatic triumph of assimilation and the "melting pot" America would have adopted a more democratic philosophy of cultural pluralism.

In the pages below I will attempt to clarify the thought and assumptions of earlier generations of sociologists. Some sociologists, perhaps still marred by the hostilities and polemics of the period around 1970, may prefer that these matters be left to die a natural death. Yet in our society there seems to be little diminution in the level of ethnic or racial consciousness, and it is both shortsighted and arrogant to dismiss the products of such consciousness as ephemeral or the consciousness itself as merely "symbolic." For sociology as a discipline achieved its maturity with issues of race and ethnicity at its core. It seems improbable that it can dispense with that core without losing a great deal of its importance as a contribution to social thought and policy in the future.

NOTES

1. David Hollinger, "Ethnic Diversity, Cosmopolitanism and the Emergence of the American Liberal Intelligentsia," *American Quarterly*, 27 (1975), 133-51.

2. Nathan Glazer and Daniel P. Moynihan, "Why Ethnicity?" *Commentary*, 58 (1974), 33-39; Andrew M. Greeley, *Ethnicity in the United States: A Preliminary Reconnaissance* (New York, 1974), Chaps. 1 and 14.

3. Lee Rainwater and William L. Yancey (eds.), *The Moynihan Report and the Politics of Controversy* (Cambridge, Mass., 1967); Oscar Lewis, *Anthropological Essays* (New York, 1970); Eleanore Leacock (ed.), *The Culture of Poverty: A Critique* (New York, 1970).

4. Charles A. Valentine, *Culture and Poverty* (Chicago, 1968), pp. 18-42; Michael Passi, "Mandarins and Immigrants: The Irony of Ethnic Studies in America Since Turner" (unpublished dissertation, University of Minnesota, 1972); Ralph Ellison, *"An American Dilemma*: A Review,"

written in 1944 but first published in idem, *Shadow and Act* (New York, 1964).

5. Fred H. Matthews, *Quest for an American Sociology: Robert E. Park and the Chicago School* (Montreal, 1977), Chap. 6; Robert E. L. Faris, *Chicago Sociology, 1920-1932* (San Francisco, 1967), pp. 107-9.

6. Stanford M. Lyman, *The Black American in Sociological Thought* (New York, 1972), Chap. 4.

7. See note 4 above; Abd-1 Hakimu Ibn Alkalimat (Gerald McWorter), "The Ideology of Black Social Science," in Joyce Ladner (ed.), *The Death of White Sociology* (New York, 1973), pp. 177-83.

8. Morris Janowitz (ed.), "Introduction," in *W. I. Thomas on Social Organization and Social Personality* (Chicago, 1966), pp. xxvi, xxxiii, liv-lviii; Matthews, *Quest.*

9. Idus A. Newby, *Jim Crow's Defense, Anti-Negro Thought in America, 1900-1930* (Baton Rouge, La., 1965); Rhett S. Jones, "Proving Blacks Inferior: The Sociology of Knowledge," in Ladner, *The Death of White Sociology*, pp. 114-35.

RACE RELATIONS AND RACIAL LIBERALISM

I

This book is a study of the history and sociology of a theory and its constituent ideas. The theory of race relations which was most influential among American sociologists during the 1920s and 1930s was that first formulated by Robert Park of the University of Chicago. Park's theory was developed during the period from 1905 until the late 1920s. It was the result of his experience and intellectual training, a way of making sense of his own life and of the world around him. At a time when most sociologists tended to avoid the entire question of race relations Park had the confidence and the creativity to develop the first social scientific theory on the subject.

Park drew upon the ideas of sociologists such as William I. Thomas and Herbert A. Miller, conservative Southerners like Alfred Holt Stone and Booker T. Washington, and upon many social scientists and philosophers of the early twentieth century, including men he worked under as a student—William James, Josiah Royce, George Santayana, John Dewey, and Georg Simmel.[1]

Despite the attempts of recent critics of Park to force his theory into their own frame of reference and then attack it as "pessimistic," static, and conservative or "assimilationist" and liberal, it was dynamic and open-ended.[2] Park believed that modern American race relations were based upon and grew out of conflict and competition among groups. Wherever and whenever the caste-like accommodation that prevailed under slavery broke down, conflict could be expected among races and classes. Within a slavery or caste system competition was limited, behavior was regulated by etiquette and rules of social behavior, and some degree of interracial intimacy was achieved. When such systems of control broke down, however, the races had to reestablish new patterns of interaction. For the most part, Park did not predict the outcome of the conflict and competition, although early in his career he suggested that a biracial system might develop between whites and blacks in the South.

An important part of his race relations theory, I will argue, was his belief that in America, and throughout the world, the competition and struggle between racial and ethnic groups would constantly give rise to race consciousness and group consciousness. This was not only inevitable, but such consciousness was beneficial for the individual members of groups and the groups themselves, especially where they were dominated and handicapped in the competitive struggle by color prejudice and discrimination. Very early in his career Park made an important distinction between those groups, such as white immigrants, who were able to discard their "racial" marks and thus enter into society and its competitive struggles as individuals, and those colored groups, particularly the Negroes and Orientals, who were seldom able to do so. Under such circumstances, Park suggested, the group solidarity and morale that appeared to arise as a cause and a consequence of increased racial or group consciousness could be a source of health for the dominated minorities. In some ways it could counteract the social and individual mental disorganization which those who were handicapped by prejudice often experienced.

My study of the ideas and attitudes of Robert Park leads me to conclude that he did not believe all minority groups in America would be assimilated. Nor did Park, despite the assertions made by some of his critics, believe that a cosmic or natural process of assimilation operated equally upon all such groups. At the same time it should be pointed out that Park thought that many members of minority racial and ethnic groups would be marked by an ambivalence and discomfort because of the competing ideals of racial identification and assimilation into the wider society. This ambivalence was especially prominent among the mixed bloods, although Park and his students thought it was best explained as a socially determined phenomenon. This approach to the Weltschmerz of the mixed blood was significantly different from the hereditarian or racialist approach which explained the superiority of the mulatto in intelligence as a product of his white "blood." Park's race relations theory did assume, however, that the mulatto had an important role to play in racial movements. When Park and his students looked at the Negro Renaissance in the 1920s they felt optimistic about the growth of a more intensive and culturally creative race consciousness among American Negroes. They were led to this understandable if somewhat premature conclusion by the important role mulattoes seemed to be playing in the Renaissance and by the fact that all Negroes seemed to be developing a racial pride and accepting a racial identity.

The first part of this study is devoted to an analysis of the attitudes held by sociologists toward immigrants, ethnic groups, and racial groups in the years prior to 1920. During those years the sociologists who were most influential in the creation of race relations theory were involved in two general movements. First, they were attempting to strengthen the environmentalist and anti-hereditarian explanation of social and individual behavior. Although they were convinced that this was the most scientific explanation and believed that social behavior was molded by the family and group experiences of individuals, they were faced with the opposition of other intellectuals and scholars who argued that heredity and innate characteristics were primarily responsible for behavior. Second, the sociologists were attempting to create a scientific sociology which would combine theory and empirical research in a dynamic manner. They were committed to a more "professional" image of sociology, in which the individual sociologist would put aside "practical" concerns in the search for laws of social behavior and societal development. The end product of this professional sociology was, for most, an improved system of social control. Since they felt that the older institutions of control such as the family, church, and community were losing their authoritativeness in urban and industrial areas, they were concerned with the development of new, more scientific, and "efficient" institutions of social control.

These two interrelated objectives of sociologists did not meet with immediate success. The racialist or hereditarian explanation of social and individual social phenomena was in some respects a powerful one. It promised to explain social facts such as poverty, crime, and ethnic or national traits or characteristics in a very simple way as the products of heredity and "blood." Whatever we may think of such simple explanations today, it should be recognized that many people have argued that the scientific theory or paradigm which explains the facts or phenomena in the simplest or most parsimonious fashion is usually accepted the most readily by scientists and thus emerges as the most popular in any competition for allegiance.[3]

Another serious problem facing those sociologists who wanted to shift the explanation of social and individual phenomena away from the hereditarian orientation was that the most "scientific" social theories already claimed to be a discovery of lawful stages of social development. Herbert Spencer, along with many other theorists, claimed that races or peoples could be divided into "higher" and "lower" races. The lower races were inferior to the higher races in terms of intelligence, moral development, institutional and political development, and scientific sophistication. Individuals born into the lower races were thought to have less mental ability, because they had inferior brains, and less moral character, because they were more prone to act instinctively. Thus, one of the most challenging tasks facing those sociologists who wished to advance an environmentalist orientation and at the same time become more scientific was to modify or overturn the orientation of men like Spencer.

I will argue below that W. I. Thomas, like Park a professor of sociology at the University of Chicago, was instrumental in the early efforts to develop a new orientation toward the explanation of social and mental phenomena. Thomas was also important as an example of a social scientist who struggled with the idea of "instinct" in the years prior to 1920. It was only in the 1920s, however, that most sociologists and social scientists rejected the loose and vague use of the concept of instinct and began turning their attention to socially formed habits.

The second portion of this study deals with the concept of racial or ethnic consciousness as developed by scholars such as W. I. Thomas and Robert Park. In the early period of American sociology up to the 1920s, sociologists were less concerned with the Negro in America than with the immigrant. Ninety percent of Negroes in the United States lived in the South and most in rural areas. At the same time, the issue of relations between blacks and whites was a source of moral and political conflict, and sociologists were consciously separating themselves from what they considered a moralistic approach to all social problems. On the other hand, the immigrant was a prominent feature in Northern cities and industrial towns, and immigrant communities seemed to be primary examples of disorganized social behavior.

During this period two social scientists, W. I. Thomas and H. A. Miller, were especially interested in the development of immigrant institutions as sociological problems. They were familiar with the European background of certain immigrant groups and with the struggles of Central and Eastern European nationality groups against the efforts of large nation states like Germany and Russia to "nationalize" the minority groups. This gave these men a unique perspective on the question of the Americanization of immigrant groups in America. They were sensitive to the historical and psychological reasons which made national languages and customs important to many immigrants to America.

In some respects the most important portion of their work for our purposes was their analysis of national and ethnic consciousness. At a time when many Americans and perhaps especially those concerned with the assimilation and Americanization of immigrants were anxious and even frightened by the nationalistic sentiments of immigrants and believed that it was necessary to detach the immigrant from his language and culture, Miller and Thomas attempted to demonstrate why policies based upon fear and anxiety would probably fail. They argued that the process of Americanization should not be forced upon people. The experience of Germany and Russia, in their view, revealed that cultural domination would perhaps intensify the group consciousness and nationalistic sentiments of immigrants and thus inhabit their eventual movement into American society.

Miller and Thomas made the argument that immigrants were particularly attached to their languages and cultural heritages because of the repression they had been subjected to in Europe. The immigrant minorities' languages and cultures and the social institutions which were transplanted or reorganized in America should therefore be respected by Americans in general and by those who wished to control or Americanize the immigrants in particular. It should be noted that while Thomas and Miller criticized the naive and narrow-minded cultural arrogance of many Americanizationists, they were primarily interested in making the movement more "efficient" and "scientific." Writers like Horace Kallen and Randolph Bourne were also critical but were more interested in developing a more inclusive and tolerant nation and in the creation of a richer and deeper American culture.

Thomas was also significant, because he was more certain than most Americans and perhaps most social scientists that immigrant culture, customs, and values would tend to lose their appeal among individual immigrants. Several recent critics of "assimilationist ideology" have centered their criticism upon Thomas as a promoter of such an ideology, but they have not read him very closely. Thomas believed that it would be most difficult for racial or ethnic groups to remain separate and distinctive in urban and industrial America. He argued that the values and customs which had proven to be functional among European peasants could only survive if they were also functional in industrial and urban conditions. He felt that it was clear from the past and present experience of immigrants in America that the competitive industrial environment demanded a more individualized set of values and attitudes among immigrants. Immigrants and especially their children would tend to discard or reject those values which seemed to them inhibiting.

It can be argued that Thomas overstated his case. But at the same time it should be apparent that he was attempting to develop a theory which explained the relative success of past and present assimilation and, at the same time, would alleviate the fears of many Americans. Americans should not grow anxious over the polyglot nature of its cities and urban areas and fear the babel of languages, he argued, because these features would probably fade away. Thomas's ideas were attacked as early as the 1920s by Horace Kallen on grounds similar to those of recent critics challenging what they feel were Thomas's fatalistic views. As the analysis below suggests, however, Kallen did not read Thomas very carefully and failed to meet many of his arguments.

The ideas and theories of Thomas and Miller had an important impact upon Robert Park and the development of his race relations theory. Park, however, was also affected by his own experiences outside the academy. He had spent several years working with Booker T. Washington at Tuskegee Institute and traveling and studying in the South. Park's ideas regarding race relations were in large part formulated during the period when he was associated with Tuskegee, but they were reinforced by his association with Thomas and Miller during the years after he came to Chicago in 1913.

In the third portion of this study I attempt to place the development of Park's ideas with regard to immigrants and racial minorities in a wider context. Although sociologists like Thomas and Miller had believed that the nationalistic sentiments of European immigrants to America were valuable sources of individual and community morale and health up until the 1920s, Park was rather unique among social scientists in carrying these ideas forward and applying them to black racial consciousness during the 1920s and 1930s.

During the 1920s a complex of events led to the growth of an environment hostile to the further development of Park's ideas regarding group or racial consciousness. Although a few of Park's students were influenced by his ideas in this area, most notably Charles S. Johnson, the great majority of his students along with most social scientists ignored those ideas and their implications. A similar fate, I suggest, befell the idea or philosophy of cultural pluralism formulated by Horace Kallen.

During the First World War, the often hysterical and coercive movements toward 100 percent Americanism were directed primarily against immigrant communities. The antiforeign passions unleashed and the anti-immigrant and anti-Negro riots and movements of the postwar years were a shock for most American social scientists. The Russian Revolution and the abortive revolutions in other European countries probably made the solidarity of all modern nations seem more problematical and made the violence in America especially frightening as a possible harbinger of social revolution. It is plausible that these events along with the horror of the war and the disillusionment felt by many at the outcome of the war and the Versailles Treaty were rather traumatic for most American social scientists. Such events certainly led many

American scholars and intellectuals to take a more critical stance toward America in general and patriotism in particular. The debunking and cynical views expressed by many American writers and journalists like H. L. Mencken were especially appealing to men and women who felt that they had been taken in by the democratic and humanitarian rhetoric of the war years.

The experiences of war, foreign revolution, and domestic violence and disruption were instrumental in altering attitudes and ideas among many social scientists in America. For instance, the postwar generation of sociologists were much more interested than their predecessors in race relations and more concerned with the origin and development of racial and ethnic prejudice. The growing strength of nativist movements like the Ku Klux Klan and the intensified movement toward harsher immigration restriction measures led many social scientists to the study of prejudiced behavior. Since they believed that both cultural and economic domination and prejudice might lead to revolution and labor and racial violence, their research was directed to discovering the sources of prejudice.

This complex of events shaped an important debate among American social scientists which was sparked by the controversy over immigration restriction. Many Americans, including some well-known social scientists like the sociologist and economist E. A. Ross and the social psychologist William MacDougall, were convinced that immigration should be more severely restricted than it was through literacy tests. Several social scientists argued that mental tests demonstrated that Negroes and immigrants from various nations in Southern and Eastern Europe were mentally inferior to the rest of the population and especially to "native" whites.

The attitudes of men like Ross and MacDougall and their use of supposedly objective and "value-free" scientific instruments like the mental tests created a crisis of sorts within the social science community. On the one hand, science, which nearly all American social scientists believed was a progressive force within society, was being used to support policies which seemed to be linked to culturally arrogant, if not repressive, policies and ideas. On the other hand, the debate over immigration appeared to be leading to a resurgence and a popularization of hereditarian ideas which threatened the environmentalist orientation of most social scien-

tists. Although the story of the debate and the impact of its outcome are more complex than this sketch indicates, it is clear that
the environmentalist orientation became dominant by the end of
the 1920s. By the end of the decade most of the social scientists who
had supported or made racist arguments about the inherent mental
abilities of Negroes and immigrants recanted and reversed their
views.[4]

A related outcome of the debate and crisis described above was
that sociologists, like most intellectuals and social scientists, were
convinced that ethnic and racial identification and group consciousness led to continued repression and conflict. This generalization fit their historical experience during the years from 1915 to
1925. A war sparked if not caused by disputes among minority
groups in Central Europe had been accompanied by anti-immigrant
prejudice and discrimination. The hopes of many intellectuals for
postwar peace and international reconciliation seemed to be endangered by the nationalistic ambitions and greed of European nations, while at the same time intolerance toward blacks and recent
immigrants in America seemed to be becoming more prominent.

Social scientists believed that the stereotypes which inhibited
ethnic and racial minorities in America were dangerous and in some
ways pathological. They were dangerous because they appeared to
lead to racial conflict and to discrimination. They were
pathological insofar as they reflected attitudes of domination and
repression among the majority group. At the same time, among
many social scientists group identification and consciousness on the
part of minorities were viewed as a pathological response to intolerance. This was perhaps the major impact of the controversies
of the 1920s upon the development of Robert Park's ideas as well
as those of Horace Kallen. Park, we should recall, believed that the
nationalistic aspirations and sentiments among Negroes and ethnic
minorities were viable and healthy responses to domination. Kallen
argued that group consciousness was necessary for the retention of
valuable cultural heritages and for the development of a rich
culture.

The failure of most social scientists to take up or develop the
ideas of Park and Kallen should be placed in the context of the
historical events both external and internal to the social sciences.
The idea of retaining or even revitalizing the group identification or

identity of minority groups was seen as dangerous and outmoded. The historical factors referred to above and explored in more detail in the chapters to follow help us to explain the insensitivity to and the avoidance of questions of group identification and identity by American social scientists during the 1920s and 1930s and the related failure of American intellectuals and scholars to take up the question of cultural pluralism during those years.[5]

NOTES

1. Robert Park, "Autobiographical Note," in idem, *Race and Culture* (New York, 1964), pp. v-ix; Fred H. Matthews, *Quest for an American Sociology: Robert E. Park and the Chicago School* (Montreal, 1977), Chaps. 1 and 2.

2. L. Paul Metzger, "American Sociology and Black Assimilation: Conflicting Perspectives," *American Journal of Sociology*, 76 (1970-71), 627-47 (hereafter cited as *AJS*); Stanford M. Lyman, *The Black American in Sociological Thought* (New York, 1972).

3. Thomas Kuhn, *The Structure of Scientific Revolutions* (Chicago, 1970), Chap. 2. I follow Kuhn in viewing sociology as a pre-paradigmatic field. Although it could be argued that Park's race relations theory was a paradigm, I will not attempt to treat it as such. Most attempts to use Kuhnian concepts in the analysis of sociology have proven to be, in my view, more confusing than illuminating. An earlier study which uses the concept of paradigm sparingly and to good effect is George Stocking, Jr.'s, *Race, Culture and Evolution* (New York, 1968), pp. 7-12, 232-33.

4. Thomas Gossett, *Race: The History of an Idea in America* (New York, 1965), Chap. 16; Hamilton Cravens, "American Scientists and the Heredity-Environment Controversy, 1883-1940" (unpublished Ph.D. dissertation, University of Iowa, 1969), Chap. 6, and idem, *The Triumph of Evolution, American Scientists and the Heredity-Environment Controversy 1900-1941* (Philadelphia, 1978).

5. R. Fred Wacker, "The Fate of Cultural Pluralism within American Social Thought," *Ethnic Groups*, 3 (1981), 125-38.

RACIALISM IN EARLY AMERICAN SOCIAL SCIENCE

II

In the 1920s the social science community as a whole began to operate under a set of assumptions or paradigmatic "rules of the game" which needs to be contrasted with those which prevailed prior to the 1920s. Up until World War I, social scientists were not confident of their ability to explain social phenomena in purely environmental terms. By the mid-1920s they tended to argue that social scientists should never attempt to explain social behavior as a product of biological or hereditary factors until all social or cultural explanations had been exhausted.[1]

The embedded presuppositions and assumptions of most social scientists in the period prior to World War I were an amalgam of neo-Lamarckian concepts. The work of George Stocking, Jr., and Hamilton Cravens suggests that prior to the 1920s most American social scientists were neo-Lamarckians and that, lacking a theory of culture, their racial thought from 1900 until the 1920s was formulated within a neo-Lamarckian context. The basic assumption of Lamarckianism, that adaptations to physical and environmental forces were transmitted to later generations through hereditary mechanisms, was seldom stated in an explicit fashion in the work of most social scientists. That assumption, however, and others which seemed to flow from a Lamarckian orientation, served important functions for social scientists who wished to explain the impact of environment and heredity upon human social behavior and, at the same time, to account for what appeared to be obvious differences between racial and ethnic groups. When early social scientists examined these groups and discovered that they varied greatly in intelligence as well as morals and manners they tended to assume that this was due to different "racial" endowments. But they were not clearly distinguishing the biological and cultural determinants of behavior.

As early as the 1900s most American social scientists believed that environmental factors such as education, child rearing, and sanitary conditions were important determinants of behavior. At the same time they wanted to explain how these factors were linked to the naturalistic or evolutionary processes of biology. The Lamarckian assumption that acquired characteristics were inherited tended (in Stocking's words and with his emphasis) to "legitimize in *biological* terms the causal efficacy of *social* processes." At a time when the model of evolutionary naturalism was powerful and appealing, this linkage was a way in which the study of social processes could become more scientifically prestigious. In the early years of the century social scientists wanted to connect their studies with evolutionary naturalism. It was only after the First World War, when the idea of automatic and scientific progress was seriously damaged, that the social scientific community felt confident enough to break away from evolutionary models of science and of social evolution in general.[2]

Since biologists and geneticists began rejecting Lamarckianism in the late nineteenth century, it may seem rather paradoxical that social scientists did not quickly jettison Lamarckianism also. Yet it is important to note that Lamarckian ideas and assumptions could be put to use by "liberals" as well as "conservatives." If the individual social scientist believed that the habits or traits being inculcated and transmitted were good, then the Lamarckian theory led him to be optimistic about continuing and accelerated progress. This suggests that men who believed in human moral progress hesitated to discard Lamarckian notions that appeared to guarantee such progress. On the other hand, supposedly inferior races were burdened by the accumulated habits and adaptations of postgenerations. Thus, the "sensuality" of primitive races or the lack of initiative and "democratic sentiments" among peasant immigrants were serious handicaps. Since they were automatically passed on through hereditary mechanisms, both immigrants and their children would find it most difficult to adapt to urban and competitive conditions where independence and individualistic habits were needed. Moreover, their past heritage of submission to priests and landlords made them poor "material" in a nation which many people felt was endangered by a movement away from democratic institutions and processes.[3]

Those who thought in Lamarckian terms tended to assume that "races" were still being formed and changed. They referred to what today are termed national, cultural, or ethnic groups as races. Each so-called race had its distinctive set of racial characteristics and temperament. These assumptions were part of the intellectual equipment of most social scientists until around 1910. Those who continued to operate within a Lamarckian framework of ideas and assumptions regarding race and heredity did not think of themselves as racists.

As Stocking has pointed out, it was only when the concept of culture emerged as a paradigmatic assumption that social scientists rejected Lamarckian ideas and assumptions. Among a small number of social scientists, including Franz Boas, W. I. Thomas, and John Dewey, there was a movement to develop an alternative theory or theories as early as the 1900s. The avant garde minority who took the first steps away from Lamarckianism in social science tended to share certain characteristics. They were interested in creating a professional social science, which would be relativistic in its approach to the customs and morals of the so-called lower races. Thomas and Boas, in particular, argued that only first-hand observation and what today is called field work among the people observed would enable the social scientist to break out of his ethnocentric biases and achieve a "scientific" detachment.

Boas, Thomas, and Dewey seldom made explicit attacks upon the Lamarckian social scientists. They did, however, as we shall see below, criticize and attempt to overturn the ideas of Herbert Spencer regarding the mental development of various races and ethnic groups. It is significant that this movement took shape during an important debate over immigration restriction in America around 1910. When Thomas, Boas, and Dewey attempted to overthrow the Spencerian theory of mental development they were also implicitly attacking the assumptions and arguments of a "scientific" nature that were being used to support the idea of immigration restriction.

Social scientists such as E. A. Ross and John Commons were writing books and articles which claimed that immigrants from Southern and Eastern Europe were endangering democratic institutions and economic and social stability in America. Although they recognized that massive immigration seemed to be correlated in some fashion with economic growth, they felt that the dangers of continued immigration outweighed its possible advantages. Part of their argument was based upon Lamarckian ideas and assumptions, but it was not a crucial part.[4]

A major portion of the material written in support of restriction by Ross and Commons merely reiterated the early arguments of men like Francis A. Walker and Richmond Mayo-Smith. These two economists had become convinced in the 1890s that immigrant laborers displaced "native" workers and led the latter to such despair that the natives did not reproduce themselves. This was the "displacement theory" which underlay Ross's continued concern with "race suicide." Ross and Commons also were worried by the high proportion of Catholics arriving in America, for they believed that the Catholics would eventually raise questions about the relation of church and state and public education which were divisive in the nineteenth century and would lead to social tensions. In a similar fashion they argued that the great majority of new immigrants were unskilled and tended to undercut the wages of native workers. This prevented the growth of workers' unions and organizations and slowed the rising standard of living of workers.[5]

Ross and Commons raised further questions about the quality of recent immigrants which were also present in the works of men like Walker. They argued that new immigrants from Southern and Eastern Europe were poor material for America, because they were inherently different and inferior. Although the Anglo-Saxon immigrants of previous centuries had been inventive and aggressive and had a strong and independent character, the new immigrants were weakest in these racial traits. The new immigrants not only were usually less skilled, less educated, and less literate than Anglo-Saxon immigrants, but more amenable to authoritarian or paternalistic rule, because they had been subjugated for centuries. The use by Ross and Commons of the term *race* at this point in their arguments was rather loose, and it appears that they believed that the traditional and cultural inheritance of peasants constituted their "racial" character.

The arguments of the restrictionists did not rest upon their Lamarckian assumptions, although they may have made some portions of their arguments seem more scientific. Ross and Commons shared a more general fear that new immigrants would not assimilate as quickly as earlier immigrants nor as quickly as necessary to prevent social disintegration. Many restrictionists believed that assimilation would not occur rapidly in urban areas and felt that the closing of the frontier meant that newer immigrants were not being subjected to the power of the American environment. They recognized that recent immigrants tended to settle in ethnic communities and remain in them. They felt this "hording" would further inhibit assimilation. In these ethnic enclaves the traditional peasant customs and fatalism were perpetuated. Moreover, many felt that the mosaic of ethnic communities would become a source of continual social tension and prevent the growth of social consensus.

Social scientists such as Franz Boas and W. I. Thomas were opposed to the immigration restriction movement for several reasons. They were less anxious about social conflict and tended to believe that peasant traditionalism was breaking down under the impact of urban and industrial conditions. Boas questioned whether there were any hereditary characteristics which made new immigrants inferior. His research seemed to demonstrate that the head-forms of immigrant children were altered greatly when the children were raised in America. He argued that if head-forms, which scientists had been certain were stable and determined by only heredity, were substantially altered in the American environment and in the city, other racial characteristics and traits were probably even more susceptible to environmental alteration. Boas included his arguments regarding the power of environmental factors in his important book of 1911, *The Mind of Primitive Man*.[6]

W. I. Thomas was aware of Boas's work and through textbooks and articles transmitted it to social scientists and the general public.

Thomas, however, also brought together the arguments of social scientists who were attacking the idea of stages or levels of mental evolution. Like Boas and Dewey he felt that Herbert Spencer's ideas regarding lower and higher stages of mental development among races were especially vulnerable to criticism. According to Spencer and his followers, blacks and primitive peoples in general differed from so-called advanced races, because they had less complex minds. The minds of primitive peoples were arrested in their development at puberty, a fact which appeared to account not only for the difficulty primitives had in learning to think but also for their child-like behavior.

In 1909 Thomas published an anthology of ethnological writings entitled *Source Book For Social Origins*. The book contained a large section in which Spencer's theory and evidence for distinguishing between advanced and primitive mental development were placed alongside articles by Boas, Thomas, and Dewey, who attacked Spencer for his ethnocentrism. They demonstrated that Spencer continually assumed that the "present civilized mind" was the standard for measurement and that primitive minds were measured in terms of what they "lacked."[7]

The articles of Boas, Thomas, and Dewey presented a functional theory of mental growth and mental powers. According to this theory all groups or races had approximately equal mental capacities or potentials. What was called intelligence was the product of the "direction of attention." People appeared to be more or less intelligent according to the observer's valuation of what they were good at and what they had previously specialized in and had been attentive to.

This theory represented an important break from Lamarckian ideas. A person's mental nature was determined not by his biological inheritance or by any Lamarckian combination of biological and environmental adaptations but by his activities. The human mind was viewed as an organ of service for the control of man's environment and the types or forms of the mind were determined by activities which led to the development of habits and skills.

The functional theory demanded that the social scientist eschew ethnocentric evaluations. Primitive peoples could not be termed dull or lazy or sensuous. Rather, they were adapted to their environmental needs. This demand for cultural relativism was clearly articulated in the articles included in the *Source Book*, and it was a crucial component of Thomas's social theories. It buttressed his own racial egalitarianism and feminism by explaining female and Negro "inferiority" as a product of their social and historical experience. Now that women and blacks were demanding more active and independent roles in society, Thomas argued, they would become more intelligent.[8]

It took over a decade for the avant garde ideas of Boas and Thomas to be disseminated among American social scientists. After World War I these men and their students played a more important role in the formation of social science theory. As social scientists grew more confident of the explanatory power of the concept of culture and simultaneously grew more cognizant of the scientific untenability of Lamarckianism, men like Ross and Commons became less influential. When a second "round" of the immigration restriction controversy took place in the early and mid-1920s those social scientists who followed the lead of scholars like Boas and Thomas were much more aggressive in their attacks upon notions of hereditarian causality and dominance in the analysis of social phenomena.

Recent studies have suggested that the antiracialist intellectual movements were part of a larger impulse toward emancipation from middle-class and White Anglo-Saxon norms. Certainly the students of Franz Boas at Columbia University rapidly developed into cultural critics and debunkers.[9] On the other hand, the relation of Chicago social scientists influenced by W. I. Thomas and his colleagues to the criticism of middle-class or WASP norms is more complex. Despite their interest in what Robert Park called the "new parochialism" of ethnic communities and questions of moral cohesion within such communities, their legacy in the area of racial and ethnic studies is much more ambiguous that that of the Boas group.

The two central figures of the Chicago group involved in the defense of immigrants against racialism and cultural arrogance as embodied in much of the Americanization movement were W. I. Thomas and Herbert A. Miller. Thomas and Miller were promoting the idea that immigrants could be assimilated without great difficulty if a rational and scientific attitude were adopted toward the assimilation process. They argued that assimilation was a process, not a conversion, and that the social psychology of the immigrant and his children was quite complex. They were attacking racialist arguments which implied that immigrants were too different or too inferior to grasp American values or to adapt to America institutions and thus emphasized the plasticity of the minds and customs of most immigrants. Perhaps their most lasting and distinctive contribution to the social scientific analysis of immigration and assimilation, however, was their ability to understand or empathize with immigrants who wished to retain or rediscover their particular cultures and languages. Several decades before American social scientists became aware of precesses of "ethnogenesis" and the social psychology of ethnic consciousness, important figures within the Chicago social scientific movement were exploring these themes.

In the early 1910s W. I. Thomas and H. A. Miller became acquainted with the development of nationalistic movements in Europe. The nationalistic sentiments and cultural revivals which became more intense in Central Europe were important topics of conversation among immigrants to America and were publicized in the foreign-language newspapers. Thomas and Miller also became friendly with nationalist leaders from Europe who often made fund-raising and speaking tours to America. When the social scientists traveled to Europe they were welcomed as friends of the nationalists and of liberation movements in general.

As Thomas and Miller traveled and visited various European nations they discovered that the nationalistic movements of minority groups were often instigated and intensified by the attempts of states like Germany and Russia to strip such nationality groups as the Poles and Bohemians of their languages and cultures. This experience gave them a unique perspective toward the questions raised by the Americanization movement in the United States. On the one hand, they felt that most Americanizationists were naive and were adopting policies which caused confusion among immigrants. This was particularly true of attempts to denigrate immigrant cultures and languages, both of which were important symbols of identity and self-assertion to minority nationalities even, and at times especially, after they had emigrated to America. Thomas and

Miller recognized that many immigrants retained a fierce allegiance to their language and culture, because they had fought for cultural independence in Europe and had friends and relatives who continued to fight for their independence in Europe.[10]

Moreover, Thomas and Miller thought that many policies of the Americanizationists were counter-productive. The attempts to force Poles and Czechs to assimilate rapidly would tend to alienate them. The social scientists shared the attitude of social workers like Jane Addams and Mary MacDowell who believed that immigrants needed to be assimilated gradually into America. Assimilation, in their view, did not need to involve a rejection of immigrant languages and cultures. In fact, as the social workers and settlement workers pointed out, the rejection of old world cultures by young immigrants tended to lead to the breakdown of family and community solidarity and to delinquency and crime.

Thus, Thomas and Miller argued that those Americans interested in the Americanization of immigrants needed to understand the European background of immigrant sentiments and loyalties and the consequences of cultural arrogance and simplistic thinking with regard to the immigrants. When the social scientists criticized what they felt were the panaceas of the Americanization movement, such as crash courses in English-language instruction and civics courses for adults, they appear to have accepted the basic premises of the movement. Yet their writings make it clear that men like Miller and Thomas and women like Addams and MacDowell were also attracted by the democratic liberation movements. By befriending and supporting the leaders of nationalistic movements the social scientists and settlement workers shared vicariously in their triumphs and struggles against cultural and political domination.

These attitudes and assumptions regarding immigrants should be contrasted with those of the immigration restrictionists. The restrictionists like Ross and Commons argued that immigrants from Eastern and Southern Europe were passive and ignorant peasants who would endanger American democracy. These immigrants had been treated in a paternalistic manner for so long that they had no democratic or independent ideas or sentiments. The restrictionists believed that such immigrants would increase the possibility of American political machines and bossism. Bossism was anathema to progressives like Ross, because he felt that it led to the continuation of corrupt and inefficient government. Ross and many other progressives wished to replace the personalized government of the bosses and machines with clean, scientific, and efficient government. The personal experiences of Miller and Thomas led them to quite opposite conclusions regarding the nature of the immigrant, especially those from Eastern and Central Europe who had been involved in democratic and independence movements.[11]

W. I. Thomas began his study of Polish immigrants to the United States around 1910. In 1908, Helen Culver, the wealthy Chicago woman who had donated Hull House to Jane Addams and supported several other liberal causes in the city, placed Thomas in charge of a fund for the study of "race psychology." From 1908 until 1919, Thomas used the $50,000 in the Helen Culver Fund for Race Psychology to collect the materials upon which his famous study *The Polish Peasant in Europe and America* was based.[12]

Thomas entered into the study of immigrants and their psychologies with an animus against the middle-class moralism which he termed "ordering and forbidding" social control. Although he did not attack the temperance movement or immigrant restriction in an explicit fashion, he clearly felt that temperance and immigrant restriction were examples of moralistic reforms which did contribute to the problem of social control. His work in the 1920s in particular indicated that he was interested in reform that would operate through altering people's conception of what was moral and what was deviant behavior.[13]

Thomas's personal distaste for moralistic or sentimental approaches to reform was connected to his early support of the cultural relativism of Franz Boas. Boas's research lent scientific support to the idea that the customs and manners of different ethnic groups were products of their historical and environmental experience, an idea which Thomas carried forward into his study of immigrant mentalities and institutions. Thomas argued that those mentalities and institutions were products of European conditions and history and that what appeared to be "innate" characteristics of the Polish peasants were products of their isolation. Once that isolation was broken down as rural peasants moved to more urban areas they began to develop new values and institutions.

Thomas's study was more than a defense of recent immigrants and their institutions. According to his theory of social development, the social disorganization of the immigrant community was neither unusual nor a product of inherent characteristics of the Poles. Social disorganization was not "an exceptional phenomenon limited to certain periods or certain societies." What people thought was a stable social situation was actually a dynamic equilibrium of the processes of disorganization and reorganization. Social institutions were constantly threatened by people breaking social rules and by social changes which made institutions outmoded. Although this "incipient" disorganization was often neutralized by the group reinforcing its social sanctions and rules, there was another typical development. Before the institution crumbled or the group dependent upon the institution dissolved, disorganization was usually:

counteracted and stopped . . . by a new process of reorganization which in this case does not consist in a mere reinforcement of the decaying organization, but in a production of new schemes of behavior and new institutions better adapted to the changed demands of the group we call this production of new schemes and institutions social reconstruction.[14]

The evidence gathered by Thomas and his collaborator, the Polish philosopher and social scientist Florian Znaniecki, demonstrated that the traditional family and community structure of Polish peasants was breaking down in Poland and in America.[15] The family structure seemed to be cracking as families were split during emigration. Family authority was seriously challenged by the young generation of Poles who were tending to incorporate the individualistic and hedonistic attitudes of other Americans. Whereas in the old country the father and the parents controlled the love life and marital choices of their children, as well as exercised some authority over the type of education and career their children pursued, in America the children demanded more freedom of choice. At the same time, the desire of most immigrants for the response and recognition that they had formerly received within the primary group of the extended family and community underlay the development of new institutions in America. The mutual-aid societies, the Polish-American Society, the parochial school, and the parish church, all of which flourished in immigrant communities in America, were necessary for the mental and social stability of the immigrant and his community.

Thomas and Znaniecki were convinced that the only meaningful organizations in the Polish immigrant community were those that were generated out of the needs of the people. Thus the community centers established by American charitable and social agencies were inefficient and virtually useless. they may have helped the individual or family unit, but they did not contribute to the community's progress or prevent disorganization. The paternalistic attitudes of many social workers, moreover, could only provoke indignation among those who had acquired a "high racial and personal self-consciousness" in America.[16] As we shall see in the chapters below, this concentration upon the needs of the community was not retained by later American social scientists. After 1920 most sociologists were trained in professional graduate schools and did not have the type of personal intimacy with the immigrant communities which Thomas and Znaniecki had gained.

At approximately the same time that W. I. Thomas began to travel to Poland to gather materials for his study of the Polish peasant, another sociologist, Herbert Adolphus Miller, traveled to Prague with a group of Czech-Americans. Miller had been in contact with Czech nationalists in America and had promoted the teaching of the Czech language in the high schools of Chicago. While in Prague, he met with Thomas Masyryk, the sociologist and philosopher who later became the president of the nation of Czechoslovakia. After returning from Europe, Miller became an ardent proponent of independence for Central European nationalities.[17]

During the early years of the First World War, Miller, at that time a professor at Oberlin College, wrote several articles interpreting both the European war and the immigrant communities of America for the general public. Working with the Russell Sage-supported Cleveland School survey in 1915 and 1916, he produced a book entitled *The School and the Immigrant*. He assured his readers that the immigrant's desire to retain his national language and culture was a positive sign of his commitment to democracy and self-determination. He emphasized that the public school was a powerful assimilating agency, but that the disparagement of European languages and customs would only interfere with the assimilation process.[18]

In 1918 Miller began working for the Committee on Public Information, America's wartime propaganda agency. He was granted a leave of absence from Oberlin and the staff of the Carnegie Institution, where he was working on the Americanization Studies series, which was published in the immediate postwar years. He was employed by the Committee on Public Information to use his contacts in America and Europe and to help the nationalists to stir up revolt in Central Europe. Later, while still working for the Committee, he became the director of the Mid-European Union, an organization devoted to bringing independence to the Central European nationalities.

In the years after the war, Miller was extremely critical of what he believed were the simplistic attitudes of the wartime Americanizationists. In an article, "The Complexity of the Americanization Problem," he attacked the arrogance and naivete of those "who call themselves Americans and who assume to run the city according to their own standards." It was quite clear, Miller argued, that native Americans needed to adjust to the immigrant at the same time that the immigrant had to adjust to Americans. Rather than assume that the learning of English was a panacea for the difficult transition the immigrant was making, Americans concerned with the immigrant's assimilation should learn to respect and understand how his loyalty to his native tongue and culture were tied to his need for self-respect. By attacking these symbols of his self-respect, Americanizationists were causing immigrant youth to lose respect for their parents and thus increasing social disorganization.[19]

It is obvious that H. A. Miller, like Thomas and Znaniecki, looked at immigrant communities with insight and empathy. Unlike most Americanizationists, they were able to move freely within those communities and thus begin to understand the needs and sentiments of the individual immigrants. Although I do not have any direct proof, I believe that they shared the nationalistic sentiments of immigrant nationalists. Their perspective contrasted sharply with that of many social scientists, especially those who wanted to restrict immigration, believing that immigration was causing social tension and conflict. Miller, Thomas, and Znaniecki were more concerned with the strengths and needs of immigrants and their communities than with the possible threat to national unity.

At the same time it is apparent that they did not question the assumption that assimilation would take place eventually. They were arguing that immigrant cultures and aspirations needed to be understood and tolerated in order to render the Americanization movement more "efficient." They also argued that nationalistic sentiments would begin to fade as public education and the economic system broke down the isolation of immigrant enclaves and the old authority structures. What was missing, however, from the later work of Miller and Thomas (Znaniecki returned to Poland in the 1920s), was a close examination of the social reorganization of immigrant communities.

Thomas lost his professorship at Chicago in 1919 after he was arrested for an alleged violation of the Mann Act. The university administration felt that his actions and those of his wife, who was involved in antiwar activities, were too embarrassing and used his arrest as an excuse to dismiss him. Although he was named president of the American Sociological Society in 1927. Thomas's career was fatally damaged. He was never hired in a full-time capacity by another university. His projected studies remained unfunded, and he turned away from the study of immigration and assimilation processes toward more methodological questions.[20] Herbert A. Miller carried his interest in the social psychology of ethnic groups forward into the 1920s. As we shall see below, however, Miller's later work reflected a movement toward more conservative social thought. Miller became more interested in the reduction of tension, and his attitudes toward and analysis of ethnic consciousness and its threat to social stability were typical of more general shifts in the social science community.[21]

The work of people like Thomas and Miller can be viewed as a response to and an attempt to shape what contemporary scholars term "ethnocultural" politics. Although some of their language may be outmoded, their basic approach and theoretical and practical goals are so "modern" one may question whether American social science has progressed much since their era.

The conflicts, at least in America, which they observed bear great resemblance to debates over bilingualism and historical and cultural studies in public schools which have taken place in the 1970s and 1980s. Those figures who argue that the schools should pay more attention to the cultural backgrounds and particular needs of non-WASP students often base their cases upon social psychological assumptions not markedly different from those which were developed by the generation of Miller and Thomas. It is these same figures who often castigate mainstream American social science for its "assimilationist" ideology. They are disappointed that there has been so little impact upon social science thought of what we can term cultural pluralist ideas and philosophy.[22]

The idea or philosophy of cultural pluralism was formulated during the period of the First World War. Like the pro-immigrant thought of scholars such as Thomas, it was stimulated by the self-righteous, paternalistic, and often naive excesses of the Americanizationist movement. Whereas the social scientific response to the coercive and repressive measures promoted by some Americanizationists was centered in the Midwest, however, the cultural pluralist response originated on the East Coast and especially in New York.

Cultural pluralistic thought, usually associated with the names of Horace Kallen and Randolph Bourne, was the product of debates and mutual interaction among figures attuned to both European developments and American conditions during the war. In the early 1900s the movement toward national unification in states like Russia and Germany had led to the suppression of many minority ethnic and religious groups. Russian programs and an intensified anti-Semitism appeared to be connected with these unification movements. This prior and contemporary repression sensitized many Jewish scholars and intellectuals to the coercive potential of the Americanization movement.

In the years between 1910 and the outbreak of war there was a continual debate taking place regarding the possibility of a Zionist nation. Such a nation, some argued, would insure the safety and survival of the Jewish people and their religion and culture. Others, some of whom were socialists, believed that all national identities and national boundaries tended to lead to conflict and misunderstanding between people. Yet the idea of a federation of nationalities which had been formulated by leaders of minority nationalities in Central Europe was appealing to many intellectuals as a democratic compromise. It would allow individual groups to retain their distinctive existence whereas both national unification and socialism would openly threaten that existence. Obviously, this was a serious and complex problem. Minorities like the Jews needed the protection of impartial state administrators; yet at times they were seriously threatened by unification movements which were aimed at creating greater uniformity among the state's citizens.[23]

Horace Kallen was one of the intellectuals who was developing the idea of cultural pluralism. Kallen believed, along with others, that the Jewish community in America should not be forced to give up its distinctive religious or cultural institutions. He was upset by the threat which he felt the Americanization movement posed for Jewish culture and also attacked the immigration restriction movement. Kallen, however, felt that all immigrant heritages deserved to be protected and strengthened. He formulated his philosophy of cultural pluralism and the idea of a harmonious mixture of national groups within America as a way of defending those heritages. Yet the philosophy of cultural pluralism also contained a criticism of the shape and form of the emerging American culture. Unlike many advocates of immigration restriction, Kallen was not convinced that American culture was something that was already formed and needed to be protected from the threats of inferior immigrants.

Kallen had first formulated his basic ideas in a response to the nativist arguments of E. A. Ross in 1915. At that time both men were teaching at the University of Wisconsin, although Kallen returned to New York City a few years later. Kallen made a general attack upon Ross's book, *The Old World in the New*, in a two-part article in *The Nation*. Ross's book was a discussion of the dangers of immigration to continued national prosperity and to progressive reform. As part of his larger argument, Ross attempted to convince his public that recent immigrants, including Jewish immigrants from Eastern Europe and Russia, were poor "material" for American democracy.

Kallen criticized the assumptions which he felt underlay Ross's anti-immigrant prejudices. Ross, Kallen argued, believed that a nation could only be unified through the imposition of a standard cultural life upon its peoples. He felt Ross was a primary example of the anxiety of America's dominant Anglo-Saxon group which, for the first time, was faced with the realization that it could not easily determine the nation's standards. Moreover, Ross's thinking reflected the national obsession with economic and material standards of success and security.

Kallen argued that only a self-enforced blindness could have led Ross to ignore the fact that America's ethnic populations had already become differentiated and that, at the same time as they became "Americanized," they became more self-respecting.

. . . the "wop" changes into a proud Italian, the "hunky" into an intensely nationalistic Slav. They learn, or they recall, the spiritual heritage of their nationality. Their cultural abjectness gives way to cultural pride.[24]

Kallen's argument at this point is like that of W. I. Thomas, H. A. Miller, and other liberal sociologists, who wished to make Americanization more humane and efficient. But although Kallen was disturbed by the "primitive" race prejudice which would lead a trained economist like Ross to be blind to the dynamic and differentiating ethnic populations of America, he was more concerned with the lack of depth, color, and dynamism in American culture as a whole.

America was developing a standardized, dull, and uniform culture, according to Kallen. The forces which many social scientists thought were leading to a more interrelated and interdependent nation were presented by Kallen as dangers. They were dangerous because ideals were likely to become standardized through the action of "devices" such as the telephone, telegraph, syndicated literature, cheap newspapers and novels, vaudeville, movies, and the star system. Moreover, Kallen was disturbed by the assumption which seemed to underlie the public school system which he felt existed for the express purpose of the blending of racial stocks into an "American race."

Kallen was attacking, then, not only the nativism of a social scientist like Ross, but the movement of the nation toward a colorless uniformity in ideals and behavior. He wanted to link the two together in his readers' minds, to suggest that they both would lead to a less dynamic and evolutionary society and culture than was possible and desirable. Kallen's favorite metaphor for his vision of American culture was that of a symphony of civilization in which harmony, rather than an essentially static unison, would dominate. A harmonic culture would provide a framework for the extension and fulfillment of national groups. "Concerted public action," he argued, would be necessary to provide the conditions under which each ethnic and cultural group could "attain the perfection that is proper to its kind."

Kallen's philosophy of cultural pluralism rested upon the assumption that each national group had a destiny to fulfill. Although that assumption could be traced back to nineteenth-century Romanticism, it is also linked to the Lamarckian notion that each cultural group is a race in the process of continual development. His assumption about group destiny connects his analysis in a paradoxical manner with that of E. A. Ross, who assumed that each group had a definite character and could be adequately described through a series of stereotypes. Of course, one can argue that it makes an important difference whether a person looks at racial stereotypes as positive heritages or as marks of backwardness. The important point here, however, is that both Ross and Kallen assumed that ethnic groups were fixed and marked by stereotypical characteristics.

Some critics of Kallen were quick to note the assumptions which underlay his philosophy of cultural pluralism. Although that philosophy appeared to be evolutionary and dynamic with regards to the wider culture, it seemed to adopt a static view of the distinctive groups and their cultures. An example of this criticism is that of Isaac Berkson, who published in 1920 a book entitled *Theories of Americanization: A Critical Study With Special Reference to the Jewish Group.* Berkson was as disturbed by pressures toward cultural uniformity present in America as was Kallen, but he questioned some of Kallen's basic premises.[25]

Berkson argued that America should be able to grow more tolerant and liberal in spirit as it matured and rejected what were essentially primitive suspicions of differences. Kallen's philosophy was inadequate, however, because it clearly assumed that each individual had a destiny which was shaped by his national or cultural group. Berkson pointed out that Kellen seemed to believe that the Jew had an "original nature" which fit him to Jewish religion and culture. Kallen not only assumed that individual Jews were fated to have a certain character, but he assumed that the present form of Jewish religion and culture comprised "the true Jewishness."

Berkson apparently was attempting to suggest that Kallen's Jewish community was differentiated between liberal and orthodox groups. But he did not explicitly point this out. Instead, he chose to connect Kallen's thought with the "traditional" tendency to pass judgment upon persons because they belonged to certain race, church, class, or sex groups. The more modern and democratic position, Berkson argued, was to recognize that such group identifications were only hints as to the individual's actual worth or potential.

The promise of American democracy, for Berkson, was to provide not only an environment of tolerance of differences, but to create continuously new possibilities for individual growth. Only in a richly diversified mental and social environment would the individual be allowed to develop in accordance with his own nature. On this basis, Berkson rejected the idea of a federation of nationalities. Kallen's scheme not only implied a false racial "predestination" but failed to satisfy the "democratic imperative" to consider each individual personality as primary. Kallen's ideas "artificially" made race a greater factor than it deserved to be. The strength of Kallen's ideas, for Berkson, lay in their criticism of the conformist ideas underlying Americanization, which had assumed that the culture of America was predetermined. Kallen's theory had assumed that the nation's future and its culture were as yet underdetermined, but had assumed that the individual's future was determined.[26]

Isaac Berkson's criticism of Kallen is representative of an interesting shift in the assumptions of social scientists who wished to defend immigrants. Although he recognized that Kallen's intention was to oppose cultural arrogance and defend immigrants and their heritages, Berkson did not believe that individuals were inevitably shaped or specialized by their racial or ethnic heritage. Berkson's defense of immigrants emphasized individuals, not groups. Like many social scientists and intellectuals in the 1920s, Berkson emphasized the possibilities for individual development.[27]

In the 1920s the younger generation of social scientists was no longer trained in a tradition of thought which emphasized Lamarckian ideas and assumptions regarding "races" and groups. This allowed them to be more confident about the possibilities for the individualization of immigrants, at least once each immigrant was freed from the constrictions imposed by ethnic or racial stereotypes.

The demise of neo-Lamarckianism allowed social scientists to assume that people's "nature" was not determined by their heritage but by their environment. Thus, they could begin their analysis of behavior by assuming that environmental explanations were the most powerful and thus the most scientific. There was a growing tendency to view all racial and ethnic stereotypes as unscientific. Such stereotypes were based upon the belief that individuals were determined by their heredity or blood. Yet, many social scientists argued, why should it be necessary to assume that hidden factors like "blood" or ambiguous concepts like "racial temperament" played a determinative role in the development of individuals?

The movement away from neo-Lamarckian assumptions had begun in the 1910s but it was intensified in the years after 1920. In part, this shift can be attributed to the desire of social scientists to achieve an independence from biology and evolutionary ideas. Many young social scientists rejected the ideas and attitudes of their predecessors as part of a generational revolt. At the same time, most social scientists who were reacting against what they felt were conservative Lamarckian assumptions were interested in reducing racial and ethnic prejudice, which in turn would reduce the potential for racial and ethnic conflict in America. By attacking the intellectual foundations of stereotypes they hoped they could contribute to the reduction of such conflict.

Many of the social scientists who were most influential in the anti-Lamarckian and antihereditarian movement had attended college and graduate school during the war and its aftermath, a time when American society seemed to be swept by racial and ethnic intolerance. In the years after the war there were several bloody race riots, a revitalization of the movement to repress and deport immigrant "radicals," and labor strife. Younger social scientists were alarmed by this apparent turn to the right in America and were perhaps also influenced by what they considered the parallels between European nations threatened by revolution and America. They felt that they could contribute to social peace and harmony by opposing the ideas which apparently underlay ethnic and racial stereotypes. The shift toward environmentalism and critique of Lamarckian assumptions was thus part of a wider movement among social scientists.

This environmentalism, however, tended to lead to a perspective which concentrated upon the individual and his development rather than the group and its needs. As we shall see below, the social scientists of the 1920s seemed hesitant to deal with group psychology and often assumed that all group movements were pathological and irrational. In their attempt to contribute to the freeing of the individual from his group identity, American social scientists became less sensitive to the problems raised by rapid social change and mobility. Their perspective made them more aware of restrictions upon the individual and less cognizant of the possible deracination amd rootlessness of much of American culture. Only a few sociologists focused their attention upon the problem of community consciousness and strength in the decade of the 1920s.

In 1924, Kallen published his book entitled *Culture and Democracy in the United States: Studies in the Group Psychology of the American Peoples*.[28] In that book he attacked the assimilation theories of American social scientists and in particular those contained in a volume in the Carnegie Corporation series of Americanization Studies. This latter book, *Old World Traits Transplanted*, was published under the names of Robert Park and H. A. Miller in 1921, although it had been written by W. I. Thomas, who was not credited as the book's author, because he had been dismissed from the University of Chicago under rather scandalous circumstances in 1918.[29]

Kallen, of course, was unaware of these facts which were only revealed in the 1940s. He was especially upset by the concluding rhetorical paragraphs of *Old World Traits Transplanted*.

Assimilation is thus as inevitable as it is desirable; it is impossible for the immigrants we receive to remain permanently in separate groups. . . . We can delay or hasten this development. We cannot stop it. . . . This is a process of growth as against the "ordering and forbidding" policy and the demand that the assimilation of the immigrant shall be "sudden, complete, and bitter." And this is the completely democratic process, for we cannot have a political democracy unless we have a social democracy also.[30]

Kallen uses this paragraph to launch a general attack upon Robert Park. It is apparent that his anger distorted his analysis of the book as a whole, for Kallen does not come to grips with the argument that Thomas made for the probable assimilation of all immigrant groups. Kallen was hampered, of course, by his assumption that Park, not Thomas, was the author of the book. In fact, Kallen compared *Old World Traits Transplanted* unfavorably with *The Polish Peasant.*

Kallen asserted that Park, and all American social scientists, were infected by the nativist prejudices of E. A. Ross. They all assumed that "native" culture was superior to the immigrant heritages. Kallen made two specific criticisms of American social scientists as a whole. On the one hand, they failed to be critical enough of the basic assumptions of the Americanization movement. They concentrated their attention upon tempering its excesses and "passed by the prior question regarding the specific nature and social significance of that which the . . . [immigrants] are said to menace." This failure led to a deeper problem. Nativist assumptions about immigrant inferiority prevented "the student of civilization" from facing the possibility that his heritage was perhaps inferior in some respects to that of the immigrant or at least no better. Intelligence, he asserted, could not be true intelligence until it could tolerate and feel at home with the uneasiness that this perspective and humility would bring.[31]

Although Kallen's criticisms were well taken with regard to the anxiety and arrogance that were reflected in the works of some social scientists, he failed to meet the arguments presented for the eventual assimilation of immigrants and the attenuation of their cultures in *Old World Traits Transplanted.* For instance, Thomas stated only a few pages before the concluding paragraph quoted above that he saw no objection to any minority group remaining perpetually in America "as immigrant group or racial element . . . if it is able to do so." Yet he doubted that such a process would occur. The "peculiarities" of such groups, Thomas felt, must be ascribed not to inborn and ineradicable traits but to a long train of common experiences.

After having stated this basic premise, Thomas went on to discuss three grounds upon which an immigrant group could remain culturally separate for an indefinite period of time.

(1) the ability to perpetuate in the new generations the traditional memories of the group without loss; (2) the ability to create values superior to those

in America, and the maintenance of separation in order not to sink to the cultural level of America; or (3) an ineradicable prejudice on one or both sides.[32]

As for the first point, Thomas argued that individuals and groups retain their memories only so long as they are practically or sentimentally useful. It appeared to Thomas, however, that all immigrant groups were "losing, *even too completely and rapidly*, their languages" and memories (emphasis added). With regard to the second point, Thomas argued that no immigrant group could claim the diversity of values produced by America as a whole. The immigrant group which was isolated would be "pauperized in even the culture which it brings." Whatever its values and strengths, such a group would be unable to create alone the values necessary in a world which demanded efficiency and "individualization of function." As for the force of prejudice, it was not serious enough, at least with regard to immigrants, to affect the persistence of immigrant groups. Although Jews had felt the force of prejudice, Thomas argued that, in general, they were losing the marks of their identity as fast as possible, and to the degree that they were successful in that pursuit, prejudice disappeared.

Thomas's general approach was antithetical to that of Kallen, because Thomas believed that American civilization was progressing toward divergence in individual types. Progress in arts, sciences, and in the creation of values in general, he argued, was dependent upon specialists whose distinctive worth was precisely in their divergence from other individuals. Thomas's touchstone for progress was science and efficiency.

The more diversified the personalities, the more particularized the products of these personalities, the greater the likelihood that we shall find among them the elements for the realization of our own plans, the construction of our own values.[33]

Thomas recognized that "representatives" of immigrant groups, and especially Jewish intellectuals, were claiming that different immigrant groups had similar social values as particularized as specialized groups.

Thomas argued that these men were misled by faulty and old-fashioned assumptions. They believed that immigrant groups were specialized by heredity as did the neo-Lamarckian social scientists whose ideas we explored above. Since Thomas did not accept the premise that group traits were transmitted through heredity, he denied the conclusion that immigrant groups were inherently poetical or philosophical. Citing anthropologists like Franz Boas. Thomas argued that scientific research had demonstrated that even the most distinct races were not characterized by any gifts or specializations. It was "easier," in his view, to explain Jewish intelligence or the tendency for Jews to be involved in trade through an examination of the historical circumstances and background of the Jewish people than it was to assume that the Jew had any hereditary aptitudes. As for European immigrants, they could not be called races at all, for they were all mongrelized and could only be classified on the basis of language and custom.[34]

Thomas's criticisms quite clearly reflect his anti-Lamarckianism. In his earlier work Thomas had believed that there were "historical" races, but by 1919 he had begun to use the concept of race to refer to biological races. Although he had emphasized the historical or cultural circumstances which determined group characteristics in his earlier work, he had not been as positive that such traits were not transmitted through some Lamarckian mechanisms. It should be noted that Thomas was mistaken that it is "easier" to explain "Jewish" intelligence or "Negro" laziness through historical analysis. It was in fact much simpler and quicker to attribute such "traits" to innate group character. It was easier for Thomas and most social scientists to think in terms of historical and environmental conditioning of behavior only after they had rejected the older framework of assumptions in favor of a historical and cultural analysis.

NOTES

1. Thomas Gossett, *Race: The History of an Idea in America* (New York, 1965). Gossett's book is a primary source of confusion and is built around the premise that the revolt against racism began in the 1920s. For instance, he states: "What chiefly happened in the 1920's to stem the tide of racism was that one man, Franz Boas, who was an authority in

several fields which had been the strongest sources of racism quietly asked for proof that race determined mentality and temperament." (p. 429)

2. George Stocking, Jr., *Race, Culture and Evolution* (New York, 1968), p. 243 and Chaps. 9 and 10, *passim*.

3. For an example of Lamarckian analysis of Negroes, see Joseph A. Tillinghast, "The Negro in Africa and America," American Economic Association, *Publications*, 3 (1902), 1-229.

4. Ross's book, *The Old World in the New* (New York, 1914), was a compilation of his popularized "science" first published in *Century* magazine. Only a few years earlier Ross's first popular book, *Social Psychology* (New York, 1908), had contained passages which denigrated the usefulness of "race traits" or "Psychic uniformities or characters" and included the statement that they were "much less congenital than we love to imagine." Later in the same book, Ross haughtily announced that " 'Race' is the cheap explanation tyros offer for any collective trait that they are too stupid or too lazy to trace to its origin in the physical environment, the social environment, or historical conditions." Ross obviously changed his mind between 1908 and 1914. In 1912 he began a friendly correspondence with Prescott Hall, Robert D. Ward, and other restrictionists and by 1913 was a member of the Immigration Restriction League's National Committee. John Commons's *Races and Immigrants* (New York, 1907) stands alone among his works in its nativist and racialist approach to social problems; it could be viewed as a temporary aberration. This conclusion seems to be obviated by the fact that Commons had the book republished without change in 1920.

5. Francis A. Walker's first articles attributed the decline of the rate of population increase in America to urbanization and industrialization—"Our Population in 1900," *Atlantic Monthly*, 32 (1873), 494. By the 1890s Walker had apparently been so shaken by the labor unrest and social conflict of the 1880s and early 1890s that he began to shift his argument and to assert that the new immigration was the cause of the decline of the birth rate. See idem, "Immigration and Degradation," *The Forum*, 11 (1891), 641, and idem, "Immigration," *Yale Review*, 1 (1892), 125. Richmond Mayo-Smith, "Control of Immigration," *Political Science Quarterly*, 2 (1887), 521, and also 3 (1888), 48, 197; idem, *Emigration and Immigration: A Study in Social Science* (New York, 1890).

6. Franz Boas, *Changes in Bodily Form of Descendants of Immigrants (Final Report)* (Washington, D.C., 1911); Franz Boas with Helen M. Boas, "The Head-Forms of Italians as Influenced by Heredity and Environment," *American Anthropologist*, N.S., 15 (1913), 163-88. A popular account appeared prior to the Final Report of the Immigration Commission—Burton J. Hendrick, "The Skulls of Our Immigrants,"

McClure's Magazine, 35 (1910), 36-50. See also, Franz Boas, "Human Faculty as Determined by Race," American Academy of Arts and Sciences, *Proceedings*, 43 (1894), 301-27.

7. W. I. Thomas, *Source Book for Social Origins: Ethnological Materials, Psychological Standpoint, Classified and Annotated Bibliographies for the Interpretation of Savage Society* (Chicago and Boston, 1909), pp. 157-59, 167-69, 174-76, 331. Articles by Boas, "The Mind of Primitive Man" (1901), and Dewey, "Interpretation of Savage Mind" (1902), were juxtaposed, along with Thomas's article, "The Mind of Woman and the Lower Races" (1907), with sections from Herbert Spencer's Principles of Sociology (London, 1892): "The Primitive Man—Emotional" and "The Primitive Man—Intellectual." Spencer was criticized not for his social or political opinions but for his scientific methodology or lack thereof.

8. W. I. Thomas, *Sex and Society: Studies in the Social Psychology of Sex* (Chicago, 1907), pp. 251-314.

9. Fred H. Matthews, "The Revolt against Americanism: Cultural Pluralism and Cultural Relativism as an Ideology of Liberation," *Canadian Review of American Studies*, 1 (1970), 4-31.

10. R. Fred Wacker, "Assimilation and Cultural Pluralism in American Social Thought," *Phylon*, 40 (1979), 325-33; Herbert A. Miller, "Nationalism in Bohemia and Poland," *North American Review*, 200 (1914), 879-86; W. I. Thomas, "The Prussian-Polish Situation: An Experiment in Assimilation," *AJS*, 19 (1914), 624-39.

11. E. A. Ross, *Social Control: A Survey of the Foundations of Order* (New York, 1916); idem, *The Old World in the New*; Christopher Lasch, *The New Radicalism in America, 1889-1963: The Intellectual as a Social Type* (New York, 1965), pp. 149, 174; Samuel P. Hays, "The Politics of Reform in Municipal Government in the Progressive Era," *Pacific Northwest Quarterly*, 55 (1965), 157.

12. Morris Janowitz (ed.), *W. I. Thomas On Social Organization and Social Personality: Selected Papers* (Chicago, 1966), p. xiii; John Madge, *The Origins of Scientific Sociology* (New York, 1962), pp. 54-58.

13. W. I. Thomas and Florian Znaniecki, *The Polish Peasant in Europe and America* (New York, 1927; 1958), pp. 3-20. The ordering and forbidding social technique was, in Thomas's view, analogous to magic. "In both, the essential means of bringing a determined effect is more or less consciously thought to reside in the act of will itself . . . ; in both the process by which the cause . . . is supposed to bring out effect to realization remains out of reach of investigation." See also, W. I. Thomas, *The Unadjusted Girl: With Cases and Standpoint for Behavioral Analysis* (Boston, 1923); Ernest W. Burgess, "William I. Thomas as a Teacher," *Sociology and Social Research*, 32 (1948), 760-64.

14. Thomas and Znaniecki, *The Polish Peasant*, pp. 1128-33.

15. In the years before World War I broke out, Thomas made several visits to Poland. During one visit he met Znaniecki, who was in charge of the Emigrants Protective Society in Warsaw. Znaniecki came to Chicago after the outbreak of war in Poland. After a period in which he was Thomas's research assistant, he became a full collaborator and shared credit as co-author of the final version of the study, which was published in five volumes in 1919 and 1920. This first edition is seldom available so I have used the 1927 edition. Robert Bierstedt (ed.), *Florian Znaniecki On Humanistic Sociology: Selected Papers* (Chicago, 1969), pp. 1-3, 10-14, and idem, *American Sociological Theory: A Critical History* (New York, 1981), pp. 185-88, 192-96.

16. Thomas and Znaniecki, *The Polish Peasant*, pp. 1532, 1526.

17. Herbert A. Miller, "Nationalism in Bohemia and Poland," *North American Review*, 200 (1914), 879-86; Arthur J. May, "The Mid-European Union," in Joseph P. O'Grady (ed.), *The Immigrant's Influence on Wilson's Peace Policies* (Lexington, Ky., 1967), pp. 251-54.

18. Herbert A. Miller, *The School and the Immigrant* (Cleveland, Ohio, 1916).

19. Herbert A. Miller, "The Complexity of the Americanization Problem," *Pacific Review*, 1 (1920), 132-38.

20. W. I. Thomas, "Report to the Social Science Research Council on the Organization of a Program in the Field of Personality and Culture," reprinted in Edmund H. Volkart (ed.), *Social Behavior and Personality: Contributions of W. I. Thomas to Theory and Social Research* (New York, 1951), pp. 290-318.

21. See James A. Aho, *German Realpolitik and American Sociology* (Lewisburg, Pa., 1975), for a discussion of the rise of "conservative" thought and the concern with tension reduction.

22. The literature on education and ethnicity is immense. A recent set of articles, "The New Bilingualism," is contained in *Society*, 19 (1981), 29-62.

23. A description of the early debate within the Jewish community is contained in James Powell, "The Concept of Cultural Pluralism in American Social Thought" (unpublished Ph.D. thesis, Notre Dame, 1971), Chap. 2. See also Alexander Duskin, *Jewish Education in New York City* (New York, 1918); Louis Brandeis, *Brandeis on Zionism: A Collection of Addresses and Statements by Louis D. Brandeis* (Washington, D.C., 1952); Horace Kallen, *Zionism and World Politics: A Study in History and Social Psychology* (Garden City, N.Y., 1921); Randolph Bourne, *The History of a Literary Radical and Other Papers* (New York, 1920).

24. Horace Kallen, "Democracy versus the Melting Pot: A Study of American Nationality," *The Nation*, 100 (1915), 190-94, 217-20.

25. Isaac Berkson, *Theories of Americanization: A Critical Study* (New

York, 1920). Berkson's book was a revision of his Ph.D. thesis at Columbia Teacher's College. He had previously been the director of the Central Jewish Institute.

26. Ibid., pp. 28-32, 93; Hamilton Cravens, "American Scientists and the Heredity-Environment Controversy, 1883-1940" (unpublished Ph.D. dissertation, University of Iowa, 1969), pp. 87-88, 100, 171-75, 208-73.

27. Horace Kallen, *Culture and Democracy in the United States: Studies in the Group Psychology of the American Peoples* (New York, 1924), pp. 209-11.

28. For details with regard to Thomas's dismissal, see Janowitz, *W. I. Thomas on Social Organization and Social Personality*, pp. xiv-xv. Evidence regarding his authorship of *Old World Traits Transplanted* is presented in Donald Young's introduction to the republished edition by Patterson Smith (Montclair, N.J., 1971), pp. vii-ix.

29. Thomas, *Old World Traits Transplanted*, p. 308.

30. Kallen, *Culture and Democracy in the United States*, pp. 211-18.

31. Thomas, *Old World Traits Transplanted*, pp. 303-4.

32. Ibid., p. 299.

33. Ibid., pp. 301-2.

34. Stocking, *Race, Culture and Evolution*, pp. 245, 248.

ROBERT PARK AND RACE RELATIONS THEORY

When W. I. Thomas left the University of Chicago toward the end of World War I, Robert Park became the dominant figure in the sociology department up through the early 1930s. This was especially true in the areas of the sociology and social psychology of racial and ethnic groups and communities which Thomas had pioneered. Through Park's students such as Everett C. Hughes, Louis Wirth, and Charles S. Johnson, his influence upon race relations theory and empirical studies continued at least up through the 1940s.[1] As we shall discover, however, important portions of Park's theory and standpoint were not transmitted to later generations of social scientists.

Robert Park was brought to the University of Chicago in 1913, largely because of the lasting impression he had made upon W. I. Thomas when they had met in 1911. Thomas had come to Tuskegee Institute in Alabama, where Park was acting as a secrtary and public relations man for Booker T. Washington, at Park's invitation, to deliver a lecture. The two men were quickly drawn to each other and fascinated by the affinity of their complementary interests.[2]

Thomas had been teaching at Chicago since his graduation in 1896 as one of the first Ph.D.s in the department of sociology. He taught courses in anthropology and ethnology and was interested in promoting and developing a "volk" or race psychology. When

Park arrived at Chicago as a part-time lecturer in 1913, Thomas was engaged in his massive study of the Polish peasant. Through his travels in Europe and in urban ethnic communities in America, Thomas was gaining the sort of first-hand experience with ethnic and nationality groups which Park had gained in his ten years traveling in the American South.

Park was fifty years old when he began lecturing at Chicago. As a newspaper reporter in cities such as Detroit, Denver, and New York, Park had begun his lifelong exploration of urban environments. As a secretary and traveling companion of the powerful racial leader Booker T. Washington, he was exposed to a range of social movements and educational experiments in America and Europe.[3]

After his decade of newspaper work, Park had begun graduate study at Harvard University in the philosophy department. At Harvard Park studies under philosophers such as William James, Josia Royce, and George Santayana and historians such as Alfred B. Hart. Neither philosophy nor history provided Park with the sense of vitality or connection with contemporary problems he was seeking, however, and his intellectual interests shifted toward sociology and problems of social science epistemology. In the early 1900s he traveled to Germany. He studied in Berlin, attending the lectures of Georg Simmel, and in Heidelberg, where he worked under the philosopher William Windelband. Windelband was concerned with the epistemology of the natural and social sciences and was part of the neo-Kantian revival which shaped the emergence of German sociology.[4]

After the completion of his dissertation "The Crowd and the Public," under Windelband, Park was unable to find a position in an American university and returned to the Boston area to grade papers for his former Harvard philosophy professors. He then took a position as the secretary of the Congo Reform Association, which was exposing the conditions of King Leopold of Belgium's colonial ventures. In 1905 Park met Booker T. Washington and from that year until 1913 Park worked as speech writer, publicity man, traveling companion, and editor for the head of the so-called Tuskegee Empire.[5]

At the time Park met W. I. Thomas and began his part-time teaching at Chicago, he had a wide background in contemporary

German and American social science. He shared with Thomas an animus toward what they conceived as the "arm chair" or deductive social science of much social science. They were also in opposition to the reformist and ethnocentric impetus in early American sociology and economics influenced by progressive and Social Gospel ideologies. Their common vision was of a truly professional and scientific social science which would avoid both the tradition of speculative sociology of scholars such as Herbert Spencer and Lester Frank Ward and the sentimental or moralistic sociologies of figures like Richard Ely and Christian sociologists.

Although Park and Thomas shared many ideas regarding the direction they wished to see sociology and social science take in America, their approaches were far from identical. In the years between 1913 and 1919 when they were both on the faculty at Chicago, perhaps Thomas's greatest impact upon Park was his ability to give the novice scholar confidence in his ideas and approach and a forum in which to express them. If Thomas was in some respects Park's superior in theoretical ambition and empirical skills, Park was often more open to ideas and theories which Thomas ignored or found threatening. Chief among these were the ideas of constant conflict in society and the irrationality and conservatism of human social behavior, especially in the area of racial and group relations and conflict. Many of these differences were made obvious in Park's initial publication for a professional social science audience. This article, first presented at the annual meeting of the American Sociological Society in 1913 and published in the Society's Proceedings in the same year, was entitled "Racial Assimilation in Secondary Groups."[6]

In this article Park attempted to cover several themes which marked his entire scholarly career. He set forth his basic ideas relating to race relations between blacks and whites in Northern and Southern regions of the United States, the assimilation of immigrants within modern society, and the significance of the rise of racial and group consciousness among peoples who were denied or otherwise prevented from becoming an integral part of society. Early in the article, he attacked the popular idea that national solidarity in modern societies was dependent upon "like-mindedness," although he did not mention the major proponent of the idea, Franklin Giddings, the head of the sociology department at Columbia. Park argued that social solidarity was achieved through both differences and similarities, but most importantly through relations and in the mutual interdependence of parts. This conception of society was central to Park's emerging approach to race relations and has been largely ignored by commentators on his theories in this area. For Park, the pursuit of likenesses which was at the heart of Americanization policies was naive and wrong-headed. He adopted an approach which, like that of Simmel and Durkheim, emphasized the organic solidarity of societies.[7]

According to Park, discussions of the Negro and the Oriental which stressed their mental inferiority or cultural differences were missing the mark. The Negro and the Oriental were simply not given an opportunity to share in that culture because of their racial "marks" or "uniforms." Rather, they were condemned to remain abstractions and symbols of their races and, thus, to remain threats and vague menaces.

Since members of these races were not regarded as individuals, they tend to become receptacles or lightning rods for prejudices and animosities. White people did not become intimately acquainted with blacks and Orientals and thus were prone to be impressed by the offensive rather than the pleasing traits of these peoples. In summary, Park argued that

Where races are distinguished by certain external marks these furnish a permanent physical substratum upon which and around which the irritations and animosities, incidental to all human intercourse, tend to accumulate and so gain strength and volume.[8]

These passages from Park's early work indicate that he was conservative in the sense that he expected that relations between whites and the black and yellow races would remain problematical in the United States. Park believed that the sources of racial animosities were found in the inability of colored races to become accepted within the wider society as individuals and in the continuing consciousness of race that the lack of intimacy between the groups created and perpetuated. This approach was quite different from that which became dominant among "liberal" social scientists, who believed racial animosity and conflict wre products of ignorance which could be eliminated or greatly reduced through education and other ameliorative efforts.

Park's years working and traveling in the South had allowed him to observe the creation of a sense of community and race consciousness among Southern Negroes. Although blacks were drawn together by common interests, the mobilization of the black community had been intensified by the segregationist policies of whites. Their growing sense of solidarity was related to their segregation and accordingly was stronger in the South than in the North. Because he felt that there was an "increasing disposition to enforce racial distinctions in the North," however, Park predicted that the sentiment of "race pride" would spread among Northern Negroes.

In his article of 1913, Park pointed to two examples of the growing race pride of Negroes. The first was the great popularity of black dolls, which had replaced mulatto dolls, and which, in turn, had replaced white dolls. Park recognized the significance of this and claimed that it indicated the Negro had started to fashion his own ideals and to fashion them "in his own image rather than in that of the white man."[9]

The second example was the increasing tendency of blacks, especially the so-called educated Negroes, to accept and enjoy the dialect verse and pictures of Negro life found in Paul Dunbar's poetry. Although the masses of the people never shared the inhibitions of the educated Negroes and found the verses both authentic and amusing, even the more educated were now finding Dunbar acceptable. For Park, this was an extremely healthy tendency as a sign of increasing self-acceptance among blacks. As we shall see below, the idea that it was healthy for blacks to transcend the apologetic literature of the pre-Dunbar period was taken up by Park's student Charles S. Johnson in the 1920s and became a central theme of Johnson's cultural criticism.

In this 1913 article Park sought to show how the growth of racial pride among American Negroes was analogous to the nationalistic movements taking place among European minorities. These latter movements were more familiar to American social scientists than Negro racial movements, and Park and W. I. Thomas had probably discussed the parallels between the situation in Central Europe and in America. Park pointed out that the Slavic peoples, especially the Poles and Czechs, were undergoing a growth of group consciousness in reaction to attempts to suppress their national languages and cultures. In both Europe and America, group self-consciousness was intensified by the development of nationalistic literature and art. Park clearly approved of these "bloodless" struggles. Through such movements, Park noted, the "minor peoples" were gaining the "moral concentration" and discipline that "fit them to share, on anything like equal terms, in the conscious life of the civilized world."[10]

Park was convinced that black Americans were moving toward racial cohesiveness and that such group strength was necessary in a competitive environment. He believed that Negroes in America had a "racial individuality" and that, as they grew more self-conscious, they could continue to discard the cultural models supplied them by the dominant white group and substitute for them "models based on their own racial individuality and embodying sentiments and ideals which spring naturally out of their own lives."[11]

It is not clear whether Park believed in Lamarckian notions of racial traits and characteristics at this time in his career, although in other articles he did refer to the concept of "racial temperament." What is clear, however, is that Park believed that what he termed racial individuality was something that could be expressed through the conscious choices of those minorities who either were oppressed or felt that they were oppressed. The situation faced by European national minorities and American Negroes was essentially the same. In both cases the dominated group would borrow and copy some of the cultural materials of the dominant group, but those materials would be

Inevitably stamped with the individuality of the nationalities that appropriate them. These materials will contribute to the dignity, to the prestige, and to the solidarity of the nationality which borrows them, but they will no longer inspire loyalty to the race from which they are borrowed. A race which has attained the character of a nationality may still retain its loyalty to the state of which it is a part, but only in so far as that state incorporates, as an integral part of its organization, the practical interests, the aspirations and ideals of that nationality.[12]

Park's article of 1913 was not not merely an article dealing with "racial assimilation in secondary groups." In it Park sought to demonstrate some reasons why blacks, like Orientals, would probably not be assimilated into American life. However, Park was not upset by this fact but went on to draw out its sociological and political implications. If blacks were not assimilated they would likely become a separate nationality. Park's use of the analogy of the Central European nationalities thus served two purposes. It illuminated the problem of racial consciousness among American Negroes by placing it in a wider framework. It also served to legitimize the racial movement as a natural product of the situation of black Americans. The ultimate outcome of the movements toward cultural and possibly political independence, Park felt, was too difficult to predict. In Europe the various nationalities were contending for a federation like that of the Swiss peoples, while in the American South there was a movement toward a biracial or segregated organization of society.

The respect which Park had for the developing literature and race consciousness of the black American was evident in his earliest articles. It was accompanied by a distaste for the literature and poetry of Negroes during the pre-Paul Dunbar period, literature which he felt was marred by a naive and pathetic striving for recognition and distinction. He saw this early period as one in which the Negro was overly concerned with proving that "he could think the white man's thoughts and practice the white man's arts."

By 1923 Park was convinced that Negroes were achieving self-confidence and self-acceptance as blacks. He believed that the Garvey Movement and the cultural renaissance of the early 1920s demonstrated that both light and dark Negroes were identifying themselves as blacks and achieving a higher degree of racial unity. Park also assumed that the "assumption" that the Negro problem must be eventually solved by amalgamation was being rejected as a consequence of this racial solidarity. Even light mulattoes were accepting the racial designation forced upon them by white America. This acceptance, Park argued, was accelerated by the Negro's urbanization, increased literacy, and ability to seek out new alliances with colored groups around the world and especially in Africa.

As in his earlier article of 1913 Park drew a parallel between the American Negro and European minority nationalities. Drawing upon and quoting George Santayana's *Winds of Doctrine*, Park claimed that nationalistic sentiments are part of a modern search for meaning and a replacement of sorts for religion. He agreed with Santayana that at a time when religion was so "vague and accommodating" nationality was, in the philosopher's words, "the one eloquent, public, intrepid illusion" which was left in modern life. Park went on to add, however, that religion was also being replaced by other "isms" such as socialism, bolshevism, Christian Science, as well as nationalism.[13]

This conjunction of Christian Science and bolshevism may seem odd and naive today, but it was an important indication of Park's approach to all forms of collective behavior. All of these "isms" were similar, becaue they replaced religion as new definitions of life's ultimate values and ultimate goods. They were, in Park's view, a partial and significant answer to the restlessness and seeking of peoples denied the opportunity for participation in the common life of their societies.

Insofar as the Negroes of America were participating in the new nationalism, Park suggested, they were more fortunate than those of the dominant races. Although the latter were not "disinherited" they were nevertheless also searching and restless. The Negro was restless but, according to Park, he knew what he wanted, which was nothing "except what he was willing to give to every other man on the same terms." On the other hand,

We of the dominant, comfortable classes, . . . are steadily driven to something like an obstinate and irrational resistance to the Negro's claims, or we are are put in the position of sympathetic spectators, sharing vicariously in his struggles but never really able to make his cause wholeheartedly our own.[14]

Robert Park's belief that nationalism and other "isms" were illusions that people found necessary was linked to his assumption that people needed to organize their lives around some central value system. He does not reveal in his writings any anxiety or fear that such movements would lead to greater conflict between or within societies. His attitude toward such movements should be seen as a corollary of his general perspective on the integration of modern societies. According to his conflict perspective, peoples and groups were perpetually in conflict for status, land, jobs, and the necessities of existence. Society was held together, then, not through any single common ideology nor through any mental or moral likemindedness but rather through an interdependence of groups which were in overt and covert conflict. Given this situation of conflict, the attempts of minority groups to raise their status would threaten groups of higher status, who in turn would tend to discriminate against the minority group. Until some sort of interpersonal intimacy was achieved between individuals, fear and distrust could be expected to persist.

This approach toward racial and group conflict was quite unique among American social scientists, especially after World War I. Park's conflict perspective was in sharp contrast to the increasing self-assurance American social scientists had gained with regard to their environmentalist orientation. This environmentalism was more consonant with the reformist hopes and antitension impulses of a younger cohort of social scientists. The general view was that racial and ethnic conflict could be traced to intolerance and ignorance. Conflict was perpetuated, if not instigated, by the development of stereotypes. Stereotypes, in turn, were merely the products of illogical thinking and inadequate perception.

Although Park stressed the absence of personal contact as a major source of misunderstandings and distrust, the more prevalent view was that education would correct stereotypes. The new anti-conflict liberalism within the social science community stressed the efficacy of education and rested on the assumption that people could be led to see that stereotypes were illogical and mythical. Park, however, recognized the resistance of most people to having their customary ways of thinking and acting disturbed. Since America was a very competitive society and yet lacked fixed status groups, Park expected that stereotypes and prejudices would continue to arise and be revitalized.[15]

Park was also unique in his approach to the rise and revitalization of ethnic and racial consciousness. He saw such consciousness as a natural response to prejudice and domination. He argued that it was part of a movement toward mental health among groups and could lead to greater social solidarity and morale. Such group solidarity was important since it could counteract social disorganization and individual mental disorganization. What many contemporary social scientists have recently discovered and termed "ethnogenesis" and "ethnocultural conflict" was analyzed by Park a half century earlier.

Since most social scientists of the 1920s did not share Park's basic assumptions and concepts about prejudice and competition, they did not explore, as did Park, the reaction of racial and ethnic groups to prejudice. The general trend in social science was toward the exploration of individual "pathologies" and lack of morale, an approach consistent with the focus of most American social scientists upon the individual and his attitudes.[16] Park, however, who had spent many years studying and helping Booker T. Washington as he developed tactics and strategies to deal with racism and racists in the South, was concerned with the racial movements which arose within dominated communities and groups. He argued that what he termed the conflict of cultures could have a beneficial impact upon the mental health of minorities. In his analysis of movements such as the Garvey Movement among urban black Americans Park expressed a great deal of optimism. The Garvey Movement, according to Park, revealed that all people classified as Negroes within society were attracted to racial movements and were tending to identify themselves as Negroes. Park believed that such social and racial solidarity was necessary for group morale. In the 1930s, when it became apparent that the black nationalism and cultural renaissance of the earlier decade had lost their vitality, Park fell silent.

It is significant that Park's clearest formulation of his ideas regarding group consciousness included a criticism of H. A. Miller. Miller, as we saw above, had been sympathetic to the nationalistic sentiments of immigrant minorities during the period up to the end of the First World War. By the mid-1920s, however, he had shifted his position in an important way. He began to stress the pathological aspects of national consciousness and also asserted that racial and class consciousness were pathological as well. Miller, along with many liberal social scientists in the early 1920s, believed that the fears and anxieties of nativists and super-patriots were pathological. But when they began to assume that the reactions of minorities to domination were also pathological, they were changing their attitudes toward group consciousness significantly.

Miller's book *Races, Nations and Classes: The Psychology of Domination and Freedom*, published in 1924, indicated that he had begun to fear not only the "dominating" psychology of elites but was equally disturbed by the "pathological charactger" of the oppressed groups. The oppressed groups, including Negroes, Jews, and various immigrant nationalities, expressed this pathology through their abnormal subjectivity and sensitivity, their guardedness and suspicion, and their aggressiveness.[17]

Miller's ideas regarding the formation of ethnic consciousness had not changed by 1924. He still believed that people grew more conscious of their solidarity when they were dominated. But by 1924 Miller's attitude toward the possible consequences of such domination had altered significantly. In the early 1910s he had been concerned with creating a more tolerant attitude toward nationalistic movements and sentiments, because he was convinced they would lead to greater freedom and independence for minority peoples. By the early 1920s he had come to the conclusion that ethnic consciousness and nationalistic sentiments, were like class consciousness. Although Miller did not directly refer to either the Russian Revolution or the racial and labor conflict which followed in the wake of the First World War in America, he was clearly affected by the threat of violence and conflict. Miller no longer felt confident enough to promote nationalistic sentiments, because he apparently felt that such sentiments were too explosive. Although he opposed what he called the psychology of domination, it was not on the grounds that such psychology was undemocratic and oppressive but on the grounds that without tolerance it would be difficult to avoid conflict and revolution.

Miller's attitudes contrasted sharply with those of Park. Park, in an article of 1923, noted that the new orientation and new movement of the Negro race toward increased race consciousness was due to the fact that the Negro was becoming awake. This process did not seem threatening to Park, for it was a natural product of awakening of the race, which was "for good or for ill . . . coming out of its isolation." As the race entered the modern world it would be exposed to all of the "contagious influences" of modern life.

The unrest which is fermenting in every part of the world, has gotten finally under the skin of the Negro. The Negro is not only becoming radical, but he is becoming Bolshevist, at least in spots.[18]

For Park, the increased political consciousness of blacks was no more surprising or threatening than an increased racial consciousness among colored peoples around the globe. In his most concise formulation of his basic attitude, he stated:

It is the necessity for collective action, the necessity that Negroes should cooperate to win for themselves the place and the respect in the white man's world that the Constitution could not give them, that has created among the Negroes of the United States a solidarity that does not exist elsewhere. Race consciousness is the natural and inevitable reaction to race prejudice.[19]

Park, in an article written in 1931, found Miller's book of 1924 interesting, although he felt it was overstated and naive. He focused his analysis upon Miller's claim that twenty million Americans were "more or less psychopathic" because of their "oppression psychosis." Park argued that the mental state of even the most ardent national minorities in the United States could not accurately be described as pathological. In his view, minorities invariably encountered prejudices when they emigrated to foreign countries. Efforts by such groups to assert themselves and to struggle to improve their status should be expected. Such efforts, Park maintained, tended to increase the solidarity and improve the morale of the minority. These involved in nationalistic movements achieved a sense of purpose and the inspiration of a common cause.

Park drew an analogy between such movements and the rise of religious sects and orders within churches. In both cases, individuals gained a sense of security and dignity within the small group which was denied them outside it.

Finally a new religious order within the church and the new nationality within the imperium of the state, tend, in most cases, to create a new society with a code and a culture peculiarly their own. Each may be regarded as a new bud on the old trunk of the social organism. It is in such conflicts as these that society renews its life and preserves its existence.

On the other hand, cultural conflicts *when they do not provoke mass movements* are likely to manifest themselves in family disorganization, in delinquency, and in functional derangement of the individual psyche.[20] [emphasis added]

These passages indicate some of the unique ideas that Park arrived at during the 1920s and early 1930s regarding group conflict and group consciousness. Minority movements, he argued, could lead to a more vital culture for America, on the one hand, and they tended to prevent social and individual demoralization on the other. One source of Park's ideas, of course, was his social Darwinist or "conflict" perspective. He believed that all societies were constellations of organized groups in conflict. Those groups which were better organized tended to have a higher group "efficiency." Another important source of his ideas was his experience in the South working for Booker T. Washington, a leader who placed a great emphasis upon race cooperation and solidarity.[21]

Although Park was aware that immigrant and Negro families became disorganized in urban environments, he did not stress greater opportunities for individuals as the primary manner of alleviating this condition, nor did he emphasize the weakness of the Negro family or its matri-focal character, as did E. Franklin Frazier during the 1930s and later. Park was most interested in the development of a group solidarity among Negroes, an idea that drew little attention from other social scientists.[22]

There is little doubt that Park placed a great deal of hope in the development of greater group solidarity and race consciousness among Negroes. As I pointed out above, Park was particularly optimistic about what he saw as the increasing tendency of mulattoes to identify themselves with the Negro race as a whole. In a sense, his theory of group consciousness, and in particular his concept of the marginal man, led him to be overly optimistic.[23]

Park believed that the attitudes of the American mulatto were crystallized in the works of W.E.B. Du Bois. This was especially true of Du Bois's famous passage in *The Souls of Black Folks* dealing with the sense of double consciousness, in which he states:

One feels his two-ness—an American, a Negro; two souls, two thoughts, two unreconciled strivings; two warring ideals in one dark body, whose dogged strength alone keeps it from being torn asunder.

Park asserted that mulattoes and most racial hybrids were possessed by self-consciousness and egocentricity. The same forces that led to double consciousness, however, led the mulatto to be more stimulated and thus, in a sense, more intelligent.[24]

It was the general disposition of mixed bloods, Park argued, at least whenever they were denied equal status with the dominant race, to compensate by withdrawing from association with Negroes and establishing a separate caste. According to Park's studies, however, this seemed to lead to physical and cultural stagnation if not deterioration. Although the mulatto in the United States had followed the general disposition and attempted to escape from the "racial coil in which his origin and his history have involved him," the color line had compelled him to take another course.

As the mulatto struggled for status in the white world, Park argued, he was increasingly choosing to "throw in his fortunes with the black and make the Negro's cause his own." The mulatto was not only the leader of the race, but also the teacher, interpreter, and even emancipator of all of those classified as Negroes. The struggle of the entire race, gathering, Park felt in 1927, in breadth and intensity, was both an inspiration and a "discipline" to the mulatto. The racial cause was giving the mulatto a cause and a career.[25]

It is interesting to compare Robert Park's ideas regarding the role of the hybrid in racial movements and the beneficial effects of such movements with those of his student E. B. Reuter. Reuter was the first of Park's graduate students to become an expert or specialist in race relations studies. Like all of Park's students, Reuter had a central sociological problem—the mulatto. His thesis was published as *The Mulatto in the United States* in 1918. It is quite significant that Park should have encouraged Reuter to take up the "problem" of the mixed blood at a time when most Negroes and especially Negro scholars avoided the study of mulattoes as too explosive an issue.[26]

In this early book Reuter approached the question of the "superiority" of the mulatto as an interesting sociological problem. Many people recognized that mixed bloods were represented disproportionately in positions of leadership in Negro organizations of all types. Those who worked within a neo-Lamarckian or hereditarian framework of ideas believed that this dominance was best explained as a result of the infusion of white blood into the lower race or, alternatively, to the fact that whites had intermixed with the most intelligent Negroes. In 1918, Reuter attempted to demonstrate that the superiority of the mixed blood was also due to historical circumstances, superior educational opportunities, and better opportunities for work and economic advancement.

In 1918, Reuter's explanation of mulatto leadership combined both the biological or hereditarian approach and the environmentalist approach to explain social phenomena. By the mid-1920s, however, the two approaches were no longer in such peaceful coexistence. Among social scientists the biological approach was seen as a threat to their professional independence. It was also an approach which could easily be used to support policies such as immigration restriction which most social scientists disagreed with. This more general movement was reflected in Reuter's books and articles of the middle 1920s. Reuter rejected the idea that there were any hereditary or biological reasons for mulatto superiority. Such superiority, he repeatedly argued, was a "cultural fact," and the explanation of all cultural facts had to be explained through sociological inquiry before biological data were resorted to. It is important to note that this assumption about the primacy of sociological explanation was what drew social scientists together in their battle against the apparent resurgence of hereditarian thought in the early 1920s. It was also this assumption and its pragmatic usefulness as an explanation of the superiority of the mulatto which made many Negro intellectuals such positive advocates of the social science movement, beginning in the mid-1920s and for years afterward. The formerly popular idea that mulattoes were superior due to the intelligence and traits they inherited from whites was not simply a "racist" argument, but one which led to very pessimistic conclusions about the possible intellectual growth or development of Negroes in general. The environmentalist social science, however, led to the conclusion that one's race did not necessarily inhibit development, for intellectual development was determined by historical and current environmental factors.

E. B. Reuter's attitudes regarding race consciousness were also greatly influenced by Robert Park. In both his book on the mulatto and in his book of 1925, *The American Race Problem*, Reuter discussed what he felt were the advantages and disadvantages of increased Negro race consciousness for blacks and the society as a whole. In the earlier work he pointed out that there was much less race solidarity and unity among Northern Negroes than those living in the South, although he asserted that in both sections of America Negroes harbored a suspicion of their own leaders. Reuter also argued that black Americans were becoming more self-conscious and nationalistic, but that that would isolate them from the larger society.[27]

In 1925 Reuter attempted to look at both the long- and short-run effects of increased race consciousness. He asserted that there were obvious advantages to greater racial unity in the short run. Such solidarity led to more opportunities for business, professional, and artistic careers by guaranteeing racial patronage. It also appeared to lead to more political power, along with more recognition and consideration. The isolation which resulted from race consciousness, moreover, decreased interracial contacts and thus decreased the amount of and opportunity for racial friction.

In the long run, however, Reuter felt that nationalistic unity would operate to the disadvantage of both the Negro and to the larger community. He argued that racial unity placed attention upon the group rather than the individual and thus restricted individual freedom and tended to retard "cultural advance" by holding the "attention" of Negroes to inferior institutions and inferior patterns of behavior.

Reuter believed that it would be to the advantage of whites and blacks to remove caste barriers, since whatever retarded the black's cultural advance also retarded the advance of the entire community.

The result is the same whether the Negroes are handicapped in their individual freedom directly by discriminatory acts of the whites or indirectly by the existence of a sentimental race complex. The latter arises as a consequence of the former and so long as discrimination and exclusion are general it is folly to oppose the growth of nationality.[28]

Reuter, at least in his work in the mid-1920s, was taking a closer look at the possible disadvantages of race consciousness than did Robert Park. Like his mentor, Reuter believed that race solidarity was an inevitable reaction to prejudice and discrimination. But he also argued that increased race consciousness could handicap and restrict the individual Negro. This was an important dilemma which Park ignored. In some ways, Reuter's arguments are similar to those which Isaac Berkson made in response to Horace Kallen's assumptions regarding ethnic characteristics. Berkson believed that there was no fixed Jewish personality or culture. Thus, Berkson could not subscribe to a philosophy which apparently restricted individuals to predetermined roles.

Park did not examine the question of whether the increased racial consciousness he saw present among Negroes was likely to lead to more or less restrictions upon the individual Negro, because he was more concerned with the mental health of the Negro group as a whole. In a sense, his whole analysis rested upon the assumption that almost all Negroes, including the strategically placed mulatto group, would become more race conscious. Park recognized, as did Reuter, that such group consciousness, like other nationalist movements, was based upon sentiment and emotion. Park, however, was more confident that race consciousness would retain its appeal. As we pointed out above, Park also assumed that mulattoes would find it both possible and pleasing to make careers for themselves within the racial movement.

The last two chapters have suggested that men like Kallen and Park were moving against the tide of liberal opinion within the social science community. Their focus upon groups and group needs clashed with the individualistic perspective of most social scientists, a fact which helps us to understand why their ideas were not more popular during the 1920s and 1930s. Insofar as their social and cultural analysis suggested that group consciousness and ethnic or racial identification should be emphasized, whether in the interest of cultural richness and vitality (Kallen) or mental health and group efficiency (Park), that analysis seemed dangerous and old-fashioned. Racial and ethnic consciousness and identification could be considered dangerous, because they would intensify or solidify prejudicial stereotypes and perpetuate prejudice and conflict. At the same time, insofar as such consciousness and identification reinforced the idea that individuals were shaped and restricted by their racial or ethnic heritage or heredity, they threatened the anti-Lamarckian and antihereditarian ideas of liberal social scientists.

NOTES

1. Jitsuichi Masuoka and Preston Valien (eds.), *Race Relations: Problems and Theory* (Chapel Hill, N.C., 1961); Robert E. L. Faris, *Chicago Sociology: 1920-1932* (San Francisco, 1967).

2. "Life Histories of William I. Thomas and Robert E. Park," with an Introduction by Paul J. Baker, *American Journal of Sociology*, 79 (September, 1973), 243-60; Winifred Raushenbush, *Robert E. Park: Biography of a Sociologist* (Durham, N.C., 1979), pp. 67-76.

3. Fred Matthews, "Robert Park, Congo Reform and Tuskegee: the Molding of a Race Relations Expert, 1905-1913," *Canadian Journal of History*, 8 (1973), 37-63.

4. Robert Park, *The Crowd and the Public and Other Essays*, edited and with an Introduction by Henry Elsner, Jr. (Chicago, 1972); Robert Park, "An Autobiographical Note," in idem, *Race and Culture* (New York, 1964), pp. v-ix.

5. Raushenbush, *Robert E. Park*, pp. 43-58.

6. James T. Carey, *Sociology and Public Affairs, The Chicago School* (Beverly Hills, Calif., 1975), Chap. 2.

7. Robert Park, "Racial Assimilation in Secondary Groups," *Proceedings of the American Sociological Society*, 8 (1913), 66-83, reprinted in idem, *Race and Culture*, pp. 202-7.

8. Ibid., pp. 208, 209.

9. Ibid., p. 215.

10. Ibid., p. 217.

11. Ibid., pp. 219-20.

12. Robert Park, "Negro Race Consciousness as Selected in Race Literature," *American Review*, 1 (1923), 505-16, reprinted in idem, *Race and Culture*, pp. 290, 297-99.

13. Ibid., pp. 292-94. Park argued that "In America, where the census definition of a Negro is a person who passes for a Negro in the community where he lives, it has been, as might be expected, the mulattos and the mixed bloods, themselves the products of the mingling of the race, who have looked forward most hopefully to the ultimate fusion of the races. No doubt Negroes are still influenced by this, as by every other motive or trend that has dominated the race at any period of its history. The disposition of the Negro in America today, however, no matter how slightly tinged with African blood, is to accept the racial designation thrust upon him and identify himself with the people whose traditions, status, and ambitions he shares."

14. Ibid., pp. 299-300.

15. See Ellsworth Faris, "The Nature of Racial Prejudice," in Charles S. Johnson (ed.), *Ebony and Topaz* (New York, 1927).

16. John Higham, "Anti-Semitism and American Culture," in idem, *Send These to Me, Jews and Other Immigrants in Urban America* (New York, 1975), pp. 174-77.

17. H. A. Miller, *Races, Nations, and Classes: The Psychology of Domination and Freedom* (Philadelphia, 1924), pp. 36-38.

18. Robert Park, "Negro Race Consciousness as Reflected in Race Literature," *American Review*, I (1923), reprinted in idem, *Race and Culture*, p. 297.

19. Ibid., p. 294.

20. Robert Park, "Personality and Cultural Conflict," *Publications of the American Sociological Society*, 25 (1931) (hereafter cited as *PASS*), reprinted in idem, *Race and Culture*, p. 369.

21. See note 3 above.

22. E. Franklin Frazier, *The Negro Family in the United States* (Chicago, 1939); Charles A. Valentine, *Culture and Poverty: Critique and Counter-Proposals* (Chicago, 1968), especially "The Pejorative Tradition Established by E. Franklin Frazier," pp. 20-24.

23. See Chapter IV below.

24. Robert Park, "Negro Race Consciousness as Reflected in Race Literature," *American Review*, I (1923), reprinted in idem, *Race and Culture*, pp. 291-92.

25. Robert Park, "Mentality of Racial Hybrids," *AJS*, 36 (1931), reprinted in idem, *Race and Culture*, pp. 387, 391-92.

26. E. B. Reuter, *The Mulatto in the United States* (Chicago, 1918); idem, "The Superiority of the Mulatto," *AJS*, 23 (1917), 83-106, reprinted in idem, *Race Mixture, Studies in Intermarriage and Miscegenation* (New York, 1931).

27. E. B. Reuter, *The American Race Problem* (New York, 1927), pp. 419-20.

28. Ibid., p. 420.

ETHNOGENESIS AND CULTURE CONFLICT

IV

Among the advantages E. B. Reuter believed would flow from intensified Negro race consciousness was that of decreased racial friction. Insofar as blacks were not mixing and competing with whites there would be less opportunity for situations of anxiety and tension to arise. Yet a few sentences later in his book, *The American Race Problem*, he noted that nationalistic unity among Negroes

arouses the fears and intensified the prejudices of certain white persons, thus increasing the difficulty of establishing and maintaining just and amicable inter-race relations.[1]

Although Reuter did not draw out the implications of two generalizations, they presented a problem and perhaps a paradox. Black unity, and, by implication, all racial unity among minority groups, eliminated friction in some ways but aroused and intensified it in others.

Robert Park did not dwell upon this dilemma, since he remained convinced that interracial prejudice, at least between those marked by color—Negroes and Orientals—and whites was inevitable. Such prejudice would continue to be generated as long as dominated groups attempted to rise in status. Moreover, he believed that nationalistic unity was a healthy and necessary response to domination and prejudice. During the 1920s and 1930s, however, most social scientists in America were not as concerned with group efficiency and morale as was Park. They were more interested in problems facing individuals. This was in part why methods of individual and family therapy became more popular, even among figures heavily influenced by Park and Thomas such as the Chicago sociologist Ernest Burgess. Sociologists and social psychologists were more concerned with developing theories and approaches which stressed the manipulation of environments in order to ameliorate social problems.

An instructive example of the differences between the two standpoints to mental and social disorganization was the approach to the problem of juvenile delinquency. In 1931, a debate took place in the journal *Social Forces* called "Culture Conflict and Delinquency." Louis Wirth, a student of Robert Park's and a professor of sociology at Chicago, presented an argument which stressed the importance of culture conflict as a major source of delinquency among immigrant children. Wirth claimed that there was an important parallel between the "social therapy" which the delinquent adolescent needed and individual analysis or therapy. In both cases, it was imperative that the individual recognize the sources and meaning of his conflict. He asserted that:

. . . [I]t is important to observe that culture conflicts are real, even if they are only imagined, or exist merely in the phantasy of the child. The significance, from our standpoint, of childhood and adolescent experiences in the family and in other intimate groups is the disposition to acquire a sense of loyalty to the values and the code which this social world imposes upon the developing personality, and which we are naively inclined to accept as natural.[2]

Wirth suggested that one way the cultural conflict might be reduced was to refashion the cultural milieu so that the individual would not be required to play fundamentally contradictory roles. This might be accomplished through migration; "family, school, and vocational adjustment"; and by supervised recreation. Another possibility, but one which Wirth did not explore in any detail, was being initiated in Europe. Some European psychotherapists were employing a type of therapy with delinquents in "proletarian groups" which sought to "bring them out of their individualistic private circle and make them class conscious, and thus furnish their everyday life with new social significance." It would have been helpful, from our point of view, if Wirth had developed his ideas with regard to this latter therapy in greater detail. It was clearly related to Park's idea that mental disorganization could be counteracted by group identification. On the other hand, it is understandable why Wirth would not want to pursue such a question, since it suggested tht juveniles could be helped by intensifying a group consciousness that most social scientists believed was a source of conflict, prejudice, and discrimination.[3]

Wirth's opponent in this debate was Floyd Allport, a professor of sociology at Syracuse University. During the 1920s Allport had been influenced by the behavioristic movement in American psychology and had written several articles attacking what he called the "group fallacy." His early work was in large part an attack upon the social psychology of William MacDougall. MacDougall was a professor who emigrated from England to America and held chairs of psychology at Harvard and Duke Universities. He was the social psychologist attacked most fiercely by behaviorists like Allport and John B. Watson, because he stubbornly held on to his ideas regarding the importance of instincts in the determination of human behavior. It is important to note that MacDougall also believed that immigration restriction was a necessary and beneficial movement in America in the early 1920s. When behaviorists attacked MacDougall it was because they considered him to be a "pseudo-scientist" and a proponent of ideas which lent support to antiliberal and discriminatory movements.[4]

In his debate with Wirth, Allport revealed his behavioristic assumptions. His concept of human personality clashed markedly with that of Wirth. Personality, he argued, was what was unique and different about the individual. Allport not only did not agree with Wirth that childhood and adolescent experiences led to the individual's sense of loyalty to group values, he was quite disturbed by such an idea. He was particularly impatient with Wirth's talk about what Allport called "intangibles" and "unseen agents" underlying behavior. Since his goal was to make "headway" in prediction and control, he could not concede that unmanageable factors like culture played a determinative role in individual behavior.

Allport argued that culture conflict could be reduced very simply. Cultural conflicts could be "abolished" by "leading" the individual to behave as if such conflicts did not exist, by inducing him to react as if he were not a member of any group at all. If the problem was one of group membership, the obvious solution was to abolish the consciousness of membership in any group. As Allport warmed to his subject, it became clear that his deeper objective was to abolish all group identities in the larger interest of reducing all prejudice. Once the individual was led to discover himself and find his integration "as a true biological and psychological organism . . . the stigma of inferiority adhering to a certain race or caste *would at once disappear*" (emphasis added).

Allport's argument is representative of the thinking of many social scientists during the late 1920s and 1930s. He felt that if individuals could only be "led" to deny their group identities, stereotypes would inevitably fade away. Group identifications were always stereotypes and existed only for increasing the feeling of superiority among the exploiters of those stereotyped. Allport argued that an effort to make individuals more conscious of culture conflict would only lead to more difficulties and tensions. Thus Wirth's ideas were counter-productive for the reduction of prejudice and also inconsistent with the alleviation of the delinquency which Allport felt was caused by intolerance and stereotyping.[5] It is important to note, however, that Allport was interested not only in reducing prejudice but in moving rapidly toward a "scientific" social psychology. Because the idea that an individual's personality was in some ways a product of his heritage was threatening to the goal of a precise and predictive social psychology, he rejected Wirth's approach. At the same time, the idea that individual personality was shaped by the cultural or ethnic group seemed dangerous, because it appeared to lend support to stereotypical thinking.

Allport's hopes for a more scientific social psychology, and his interest in the reduction of prejudice and conflict, led him to take a position in important ways antithetical to that of Robert Park. Park's conflict orientation and his belief that racial and ethnic groups would remain in competition with dominant groups within society led him to study group consciousness as a recurrent phenomenon. Park did not challenge the stereotypes whites had regarding Negroes or Orientals, because he was more interested in understanding how they worked than in their danger. Allport felt that ethnic groups and racial groups could only be seen in general terms as myths and also believed that the idea of culture was an "unseen agent."

During the late 1920s the idea that all stereotypes were based upon myth and pseudo-scientific thinking became popular among most social scientists. If all cultural identifications were based upon irrational thinking, it was clear that social scientists should stop identifying individuals by race or ethnic group. Insofar as individual members of ethnic and racial groups thought of themselves as members of races or distinctive ethnic groups they were deluding themselves. In a similar fashion, members of such groups who supported the idea of continued group identification would be viewed as not only unscientific but as counter-productive forces. They were directly or indirectly inhibiting the growth of tolerance by perpetuating irrational and stereotypical behavior.[6]

The attitude of Robert Park toward minority group consciousness was much more sympathetic than that expressed by social scientists like Floyd Allport. Those social scientists who were most interested in opposing what they considered to be the pseudo-scientific thinking of nativists and immigration restrictionists of the 1920s were not particularly interested in how the groups who were dominated were to deal with that domination. Park, by way of contrast, did not approach racial or ethnic prejudice as an outgrowth of irrational or mythical thinking, because he believed that prejudice grew out of the conflict between groups struggling for existence and status. Consequently, he did not express much concern, at least in his published works, with the reduction of prejudice. As we have seen above, Park did not believe that group identification and consciousness were products of unscientific or mythical thinking. If nationalism or racial pride was based upon illusion, that did not make the pride any less real or less a healthy reaction to prejudice. This was one of the major points of difference between his approach and that of most social scientists.[7]

Park's ideas with regard to group efficiency and morale were developed out of his Darwinist or conflict perspective. If we read his articles closely, however, it becomes apparent that his ideas with regard to the beneficial effects of group identification were based, at least in part, upon his own empirical studies and life experiences. Park liked to present a public image of himself as a hardheaded man who had lost all his reformist illusions back when he was a muckraking reporter in the 1890s. But at least in one instance, he was involved in reform which failed and left him disillusioned. This sense of loss is most marked, in fact, because it is absent from almost all of his published works.

From 1922 to 1924, Park was the president of the National Community Center Association, which had its headquarters in Chicago. The general objective of this association was to strengthen neighborhood communities and to present an alternative to the political machines which seemed to dominate local government. In 1925, the University of Chicago Press published a book entitled *The City*, which contained several essays by Park. These essays reveal Park's personal philosophy of democratic city life as no others do. Because he has reflected upon the meaning of the failure of the Community Center movement, he comes closer to a criticism of American culture in them than anywhere else in his work.

What was wrong with American cities, Park argued, was that they were social failures. Local studies in Chicago had indicated that community efficiency and competence were not correlated with the number of competent people within that community. Park's research and personal experience had led him to conclude that professional people were not involved in the political and moral life of the city, a fact which he traced to their tendency to live in suburbs. The professionals had only a dilettantish and "sporting interest" in local politics and the problems of the local community.

Although Park was disappointed with the escapism of the professional class, he felt that the American people as a whole were becoming romantic. When people were not working, they were involved in a restless search for excitement and sought to escape from what was felt to be the dull routine of life at home and in the local community. He found evidence of this romantic quest in the changing culture in the cities, including dance halls, jazz parlors, political revolution, religious millennialism, automobiles, and airplanes.

We are everywhere hunting the bluebird of romance. . . . The new devices of locomotion have permitted millions of people to realize, in actual life, flights of which they had only dreamed of previously. But this physical mobility is but the reflection of a corresponding mental instability. This restlessness and thirst for adventure is, for the most part, barren and illusory, because it is uncreative. We are seeking to escape from a dull world instead of turning back upon it to transform it.[8]

Park contrasted the community inefficiency of most city areas with the efficiency of the immigrant enclaves. The immigrant community existed, he argued, to enable the immigrant to live. It was therefore structured to meet his needs for security, recreation, belongingness, and affection. Most immigrant communities included religious organizations and mutual aid and welfare organizations which increased community solidarity. Each tended to have its own businesses, clubs, lodges, restaurants, gathering places, and press. The important point was that all of these institutions provided a full round of life and enabled the immigrant to withstand the culture shock he received in America.

Park was disappointed that America was not developing a common culture. Such a culture could lead to the solidarity and moral consensus that were lacking within most American communities. He recognized that America was not likely to develop a sense of community because of the pressures toward what W. I. Thomas had called "individualization." What appeared to be best for the individual, Park suggested, from the point of view of society and community was leading to social disorganization. American society was becoming atomized, and the habits upon which stable communities were based could not survive.

In a paper which for some reason remained unpublished, Park attempted to come to grips with the difference between "culture" and "civilization." America was becoming a *civilization*, which was merely an aggregate of people "who use the same artifacts and who have no solidarity at all." *Culture*, on the other hand, was the product and function of groups that could act collectively. Culture grew up where collective action was needed. In America, Park argued, the atomization of life was being intensified by the automobile, the newspaper, and the motion pictures. As people moved to cities they became emancipated and more cosmopolitan. But what seemed to be an emancipation to individual migrants and their families also disrupted the communities they left behind and the communities into which they moved. Migration even disrupted the individual migrants themselves and particularly the younger generation.[9]

Park's general argument about the destruction of community ties and social disorganization in America places his attitudes toward the growth of racial and ethnic consciousness among immigrants and blacks into a wider and more meaningful context. His argument, as expressed in his essays and articles of the 1920s, was that community efficiency was closely tied to group consciousness and to the cohesion that was aroused by prejudice. His sympathetic view of minority group communities was an implicit, and occasionally explicit, criticism of American society outside ethnic and racial enclaves for its excessive individualism. His writings exhibited a growing discomfort with the lack of a genuine moral order within the wider society.

The moral order that marked isolated cultures, he felt, could not be reconstituted within America, which had at best a civilization rather than a common culture. Civilizations could only be organized around patriotism and a shifting public opinion. In America, he stated:

There is a political order based not on custom but on public opinion which is in constant change and under which laws are hard to enforce. To stop automobile thefts, for instance, in the city of Chicago, we virtually have to organize a crusade.[10]

As Park grew more discomforted with the "nondescript" and "formless" movement of American life, his earlier hopes grew dim. Although Park had once hoped that the immigrant communities would prove to be a model for community reorganization, by the 1930s his belief in what he termed the "new parochialism" which would run counter to romanticism and escapism seemed rather utopian.[11]

Park, however, was in part only sensing the decline of the liberal intellectual community of Chicago and shared the loss of confidence of those progressives who had hoped to bring rationality and efficiency to urban American cities. At least one of Park's students, Charles S. Johnson, did not share his mentor's pessimism. During the years when Johnson was research director for racial commissions and for the Urban League (1919 to 1928) and in his years at the black college Fisk University as chairman of its social science department (1928 to 1946), his articles and books revealed his own creative use of the standpoint and orientation of Parkian sociology.

Johnson was a Negro from Virginia who took his undergraduate degree at Virginia Union University. He came to Chicago to study under Park in the late 1910s and took a second bachelor's degree at the University of Chicago in 1917. From 1919 to 1921 he was the associate executive secretary of the Chicago Commission on Race Relations, which had been formed at the request of the governor of Illinois to investigate the causes and implications of the Chicago race riot of 1919. Johnson's role with the commission was to gather and analyze the research data and help write the final report.[12]

The conclusions of the commission, published in 1922 as *The Negro in Chicago*, emphasized that the riot was in many respects the outgrowth of years of discrimination, prejudice, and racial conflict in the city. The migration of Negroes to Chicago during the First World War had led to an intensification of the friction between Negro workers and other groups, including immigrants and migrants from areas outside of Chicago. The growing Negro population competed with other groups for housing as well as jobs, and the pressure of population increases tended to break down what had been established boundaries which divided groups along ethnic and racial lines. Instrumental in the instigation of violence were youth groups and gangs, especially those of the Irish community, who were often encouraged by older residents to harass Negroes. Also, the white press of Chicago had fanned the flames of anti-Negro sentiment through biased and irresponsible reports of Negro crime and vice.[13]

The report bore the marks of Robert Park's emphasis on the problems of conflict for jobs and living space as major factors underlying race problems. When Johnson left Chicago to become the head of the National Urban League's department of research, he continued to deal with the problems caused by Negro migration to cities. In his role as editor of the League's national publication, *Opportunity*, from 1923 to 1928, he began to take an active part in the Negro Renaissance and to emphasize the cultural aspect of that migration. While he was editing the magazine, it provided a valuable showcase and outlet for talented writers and artists, including many who are generally associated with the Harlem Renaissance. At the same time, *Opportunity* contained the most advanced and liberal opinion with regard to the American Negro and the latest developments in social science.

As we have noted in earlier chapters, during the mid-1920s

American social scientists moved toward a more rigorous environmentalism as sociologists and others attacked the hereditarian and racist ideas and assumptions of those supporting immigration restriction and other nativist movements. Johnson's editorials and the articles of the liberal social scientists he solicited kept the readers of the magazine abreast of the latest research pertinent to the controversy centered on immigration restriction.

A good example of the movement toward an environmentalist orientation was the controversy over mental testing. The mental tests of "intelligence" popularized during World War I had been interpreted by some social scientists as scientific proof of the mental inferiority of Negroes and certain groups of immigrants from Eastern and Southern Europe. Men like Johnson and Horace Mann Bond, who was also a student of Park's at Chicago, pointed out that the tests demonstrated that Northern Negroes consistently scored higher on the tests than Southern whites. This suggested that the tests were measuring environmental and educational differences rather than any "innate" mental abilities.[14]

Charles Johnson was also an important figure, because he formulated a more positive and sympathetic view of the Southern Negro migrant to the urban North and of his cultural heritage. His own Virginia background was perhaps one factor which led him to this point of view, but more important was his vision of the possibilities of the Negro cultural movement as a source of racial pride and solidarity. Johnson, however, was not a custodian of culture who attempted to channel the efforts of artists and writers in any *a priori* direction. At the same time, it is clear that he was most interested in those cultural products expressive of the culture of the folk which would tend to break down the unitary image of the black American.[15]

Johnson's attitudes toward the folk culture of Negroes reveal an interesting shift away from the attitudes of most middle-class Negro intellectuals. Other intellectuals, including sociologists such as W.E.B. Du Bois and George Edmund Haynes, had also insisted that a unitary image or stereotype of Negroes was faulty, but they usually argued that it was the black middle class that deserved greater recognition. They felt that if whites would recognize that some Negroes were approaching and at times exceeding white standards in art, morality, and energy, white prejudice toward

Negroes would be weakened. Johnson argued that this approach to the reduction of white prejudice was incorrect, elitist, and moralistic. Negro groups varied by custom and culture patterns. In some ways, he suggested, different cities and regions were developing varied patterns of life.[16]

Johnson believed that the most important racial distinction was that between the small articulate minority and the folk or peasant majority. Like Robert Park, he found the latter to be more interesting, for it had made the more significant and original contributions to music, folklore, and dance. The educated minority might have made the more conscious and deliberate contributions to arts and letters, but those contributions were, in his view, seriously flawed by self-consciousness and by their imitation of white models. The middle-class artist had been stifled by the need to prove that he was "just like white people." In the 1920s, however, the past pattern of imitation and constricting self-consciousness was breaking down. Negro writers were rising above their former self-defensiveness and were, at least at times, becoming self-critical and critical of white culture and standards also.

The discovery of the folk Negro was an exciting phenomenon, Johnson thought, because it signaled a new attitude toward the repressed materials of Negro life and culture. Most educated Negroes were afraid to deal with, and bitterly opposed those who dared to deal with, "Negro dialect, and folk songs, and anything that revived the memory of slavery." The rise of the healthy new attitudes toward the repressed marked the decline of the faulty views of the race moralists. Their cultural standards had been based upon an implicit "sociology." That sociology had assumed that if the more educated and cultured Negroes were emphasized in works of fiction, the dominant white groups would have a better opinion of all Negroes. Johnson argued that this was poor strategy, because it involved an unhealthy denial of reality and led to the replacement of one stereotype with another.[17]

Charles Johnson's beliefs regarding the impact of the discovery of the folk Negro did not merely have implications for racial strategy and the breaking down of stereotypes. He asserted that that discovery was leading to the emancipation of Negro and white writers and artists. Negroes were being recognized as rounded human beings and as characters "capable of living by their own charm and power." Thus, art promised, in Johnson's view, to merge with science in a common movement toward a new vision of the Negro in his diversity and complexity.

Johnson's ideas and attitudes were most appealing to the Negro cultural critic Alain Locke. Locke's criticism is interesting and in some ways unique, because he attempted to balance in his mind at the same time two sets of ideas which are usually considered to be mutually contradictory or antithetical. The first set of ideas centered around the idea of the cultural uniqueness of the American Negro. Locke did not make use of the concept of racial soul or genius, but he believed that the Negro had a unique contribution to make to American culture. The second set of ideas was based on his belief on the idea of environmentalism. He supported the modern social scientific view that what distinguishes human beings from each other could be traced to the impact of environmental factors such as education, training in families and intimate groups, and their location in an ecological order.

Locke was able to keep these two ideas in some sort of balance, because he was defending and promoting Negro culture not as something already formed, but as a culture in the process of development and emergence. He shared Charles Johnson's belief that the central dynamic of the Negro Renaissance was its recognition of the diversity of Negro life and art. The Negro culture he anticipated would be derived from the release of energy and the development of consciousness of the Negro in new environments. In environments such as Harlem, he suggested, there would be a rediscovery and a reworking of the folk heritage of the Southern Negro.

Locke is an important figure, because he carried on the attempt to merge the ideas of cultural uniqueness and environmentalism when most social scientists gave up and adopted assimilationist ideas or remained silent. Charles Johnson left New York for Fisk and turned to sociological research, which although valuable in many ways, often lacked the excitement and insightfulness of his earlier work. As we noted above, Horace Kallen appeared to lose his interest in cultural pluralism after the mid-1920s. Because Locke came to grips with the idea of environmentalism, he made a more lasting contribution to the idea of cultural pluralism than Kallen, whom he had known when they were both students at Harvard University around 1910.

An important difference between Kallen and Locke was that they were operating in different time perspectives. Locke was promoting the idea of an emergent Negro culture. Kallen, on the other hand, was in large part defending the retention of established cultures or heritages. In his vision of the drama of Negro life and culture, Locke viewed the players in the process of taking on new, more rounded and human roles while rejecting old restricting roles. Kallen, at least during the period from 1915 until 1925, saw the repression of American immigrant and Jewish culture as another episode in the centuries-old tragedy of intolerance. Yet for many immigrants and for the Negro, whom Kallen ignored, the 1920s were a time for the bursting of old bonds and the breaking of old stereotypes.[18]

Alain Locke, like Charles Johnson, was defending the idea of the historical and psychological uniqueness of the Negro experience in America. Their cultural criticism, which included the literature of social science and history as well as arts and letters, was centered around what they called realism. Realistic literature and social science both uncovered the repressed content of the Negro and the American past. Art and literature, as well as social science and history, were most significant when they brought into consciousness the experience and consequences of the Negro past. Both Locke and Johnson were not simply interested in the uncovering or debunking of past myths or stereotypes, however, but in how Negro and white artists and scholars were experiencing and refashioning the past.[19]

Locke, who sustained his interest in cultural criticism after Johnson moved from New York to Fisk University, continued to call for realism in art and social science during the 1930s. He argued that what American Negroes and whites needed was an unflinching examination of the diversity of Negro life at all social levels and in all circumstances. Artists and writers could liberate the Negro from constricting stereotypes, especially those of ministrelry and sentimentality, and social science needed to continue to move away from propaganda and moralism. Locke believed that the propagandistic approach to the Negro, the idea that the Negro constituted a unique problem, had been at the center of the controversies between whites and blacks, liberals and conservatives, since the Civil War. If there was a "Negro problem," he argued, social scientists should not approach it as one which was essentially different from the problems of American society and culture as a whole.[20]

Locke believed that the most encouraging mark of the movement away from the traditional sentimental images of the Negro was the growing ability of the artist and writer to show a true respect for the folk Negro and the migrant to the city. In the early 1930s, he looked back at the period of the Harlem Renaissance as one in which the Negro had been a fad and an exotic. Many individual Negro artists, he believed, had become too "exhibitionistic." In some ways Locke himself had, in the enthusiasm of the mid-1920s, played a role in this movement toward "primitivism," although he never clearly admitted it.[21] Nevertheless, by the mid-1930s, Locke was achieving a deeper understanding of the difficulties of developing more realistic images of the black American. The work of the Negro and white artist and social scientist, he felt, was growing more sober and dignified, but their dignity and sobriety were not

the stiff pose and starched trappings of the moralist . . . but instead the simple, unaffected dignity of sympathetic and often poetic realism and the sobriety of the artist who loves and respects his subject-matter. It was one thing to inveigh against the Negro stereotypes in fiction, drama, art and sociology, it was quite another to painfully reconstruct from actual life truer, livelier, more representative substitutes.[22]

Locke was particularly impressed with the work of the sociology department at the University of North Carolina and the theoretical contributions of the students of Robert Park to the understanding of the life and culture of the Southern Negro. Howard W. Odum and Guy B. Johnson had made particularly stimulating studies of the music and folk tales of the rural and small-town Negro. It is interesting to note that it was only after Guy Johnson, who had studied under Park and received an M.A. from the University of Chicago in 1922, came to North Carolina in the mid-1920s that Odum, who had been there for many years, returned to the study of the folk Negro, the subject of much of his early work in the period around 1910.[23]

Locke also found the work of Park and his students most interesting. E. Franklin Frazier's work on the development of Negro family patterns illuminated the diversity of historical experiences of

Negroes in the United States. Charles Johnson was revealing promise as an interpreter of the mind and culture of the rural Negro in books such as *The Shadow of the Plantation*. Locke was particularly interested in the movement of Robert Park's thought toward the idea of cultural fusion.[24]

Park and Locke shared an interest in the problem of cultural fusion and a curiosity about the implications of the worldwide mixture of races and culture. Park believed that only through a comparative study of situations where racial and cultural mixtures were occurring would American sociologists begin to understand race relations.[25] Locke was interested in studies of cultural fusion whenever they promised to make the situation of the American Negro and cultural pluralism in America more intelligible.

In retrospect, Park and Locke were grappling with problems which still demand close examination. Neither man, however, was able to develop a body of students or a research tradition which led to the elaboration or further development of their ideas regarding cultural frontiers and cultural fusion. Social scientists in the 1930s and 1940s did not share their concern with such problems.[26] Students of race relations moved toward a liberal activism which led them to focus upon what they believed were the unique problems of America. A concern with reducing racial conflict took precedence over other problems and, in some ways, made the problem of cultural fusion and frontiers appear to be trivial. In their efforts to countract prejudice and thus racism, most social scientists adopted an assimilationist viewpoint. The thrust of the ideas of Park and Locke were, given this general atmosphere, neglected when they were not viewed as pessimistic and conservative.[27]

NOTES

1. E. B. Reuter, *The American Race Problem* (New York, 1927), p. 420.

2. Louis Wirth, "Culture Conflict and Misconduct," *Social Forces*, 9 (1931), 492.

3. Ibid., p. 492.

4. Floyd Allport, "The Group Fallacy in Relation to Social Science," *AJS*, 19 (1924), 688-706; "Group and Institution as Concept in a Natural Science of Social Phenomena," *PASS*, 22 (1928), 83-99. See William MacDougall, *Is American Safe for Democracy?* (New York, 1921).

5. Floyd Allport, "Culture Conflict Versus the Individual as Factors in Delinquency," *Social Forces*, 9 (1931), 492-97.

6. Ashley Montague, *Man's Most Dangerous Myth* (New York, 1942; revised edition, 1964), p. 345.

7. Robert Park, "Negro Race Consciousness as Revealed in Race Literature," *American Review*, 1 (1923), reprinted in idem, *Race and Culture* (New York, 1964), pp. 299-300.

8. Robert Park, "Community Organization and the Romantic Tember," *Social Forces*, 3 (1925), reprinted in idem, *Human Communities: The City and Human Ecology* (Glencoe, Ill., 1952), pp. 64-65, 68-69.

9. Robert Park, "Culture and Civilization," unpublished paper, collected in idem, *Race and Culture*, pp. 20-22.

10. Ibid., p. 21.

11. Park, "Community Organization," p. 72.

12. Edwin Embree, *Thirteen Against the Odds* (New York, 1946), pp. 47-70.

13. Chicago Commission on Race Relations, *The Negro in Chicago* (Chicago, 1922).

14. Charles S. Johnson, editorials in *Opportunity*, 2 (1924), 3-4, 194; Horace Mann Bond, "What the Army 'Intelligence' Tests Measured," *Opportunity*, 2 (1924), 197-202.

15. Charles S. Johnson, "Introduction," *Ebony and Topaz: A Collectanea* (New York, 1927), pp. 11-13.

16. Charles S. Johnson, "The New Frontage on American Life," in Alain Locke (ed.), *The New Negro: An Interpretation* (New York, 1927), pp. 278-98.

17. Johnson, "Introduction," p. 12.

18. See the analysis of the time perspective of "new" and "old" peoples in Everett C. Hughes, "New Peoples," in Andrew Lind (ed.), *Race Relations in World Perspective* (Honolulu, 1954), pp. 95-115.

19. Johnson, "Introduction"; Alain Locke, "The Eleventh Hour of Nordicism," *Opportunity*, 13 (1935), 8, 46-48, 59; Alain Locke, "1928: A Retrospective Review," *Opportunity*, 7 (1929), 8-11.

20. Alain Locke, "Black Truth and Black Beauty," *Opportunity*, 11 (1933), 14.

21. Alain Locke, "The Saving Grace of Realism," *Opportunity*, 12 (1934), 8-9. In 1928, Locke had argued that the primitive and pagan Negro was a popular theme in literature and culture, because Americans were rediscovering "senses and the instincts." By the early 1930s, however, he had drawn back from that position. See idem, "Beauty Instead of Ashes," *The Nation*, 126 (1928), 432-34. Compare Wallace Thurman, "Nephews of Uncle Remus," *The Independent*, 109 (1927), 296-98, and idem, "Negro Artists and the Negro," *The New Republic*, 52 (1927), 37-39.

22. Locke, "The Saving Grace of Realism," p. 8.

23. The reactions of Locke, C. S. Johnson, and Park are contained in the following: "1928: A Retrospective Review," pp. 9-10; idem, "Black Truth and Black Beauty," pp. 14-15; Johnson, "Introduction," p. 9; Robert Park, book review in *AJS*, 33 (1928), 989-95. The books reviewed by Park included Howard W. Odum, *Rainbow Round My Shoulder: The Blue Trail of Black Ulysses* (Indianapolis, Ind., 1928); Howard W. Odum and Guy B. Johnson, *Negro Workaday Songs* (Chapel Hill, N.C., 1926); Newbell Niles Puckett, *Folk Beliefs of the Southern Negro* (Chapel Hill, N.C., 1926); E.C.L. Adams, *Congaree Sketches* (Chapel Hill, N.C., 1927); Alain Locke and Montgomery Gregory (eds.), *Plays of Negro Life* (New York, 1927); Countee Cullen (ed.), *Caroling Dusk* (New York, 1927); James Weldon Johnson, *God's Trombones* (New York, 1927); and R. Nathaneil Dett (ed.), *Religious Folk-Songs of the Negro* (Hampton, Va., 1927).

24. Locke, "The Eleventh Hour of Nordicism," p. 46.

25. John Higham, *Send These to Me, Jews and Other Immigrants in Urban America* (New York, 1975), pp. 214-17; Fred H. Matthews, *Quest for an American Sociology; Robert E. Park and the Chicago School* (Montreal, 1977), pp. 164-74.

26. The sociologists closest Park's viewpoint were E. Franklin Frazier, *Race and Culture Contacts in the Modern World* (New York, 1957), and E. C. Hughes and Helen MacGill Hughes, *Where Peoples Meet, Racial and Ethnic Frontiers* (Glencoe, Ill., 1952).

27. James A. Aho, *German Realpolitik and American Sociology, An Inquiry into the Sources and Political Significance of the Sociology of Conflict* (Lewisburg, Pa., 1975), pp. 279-314.

THE CLASH OF PARADIGMS: PARK AND MYRDAL

V

During the 1930s, as American intellectuals and scholars became more aware of the racist ideology of the Nazis and fascists, the idea that ethnic consciousness and identification was dangerous and a source of intolerance was reinforced. Moreover, during the late 1920s and 1930s, American anthropologists became more prominent in the formation of liberal opinion in the area of race and ethnicity. The dominant school of anthropologists in America, that of Franz Boas and his students, popularized the idea that there were no biological races. The various peoples of the world were not different in any important way, they held, and most population groups were distinguished only by overlapping frequency curves when tested by anthropologists or geneticists. It is plausible that since many of Boas's students were Jewish or of Jewish origin, they were moved toward a more activist and vocal position by the fate of Jewish scholars and intellectuals in Nazi Germany, as well as by the anti-Semitic legislation passed under Hitler's regime. When the Nazis removed Jewish scholars from the schools and universities in 1933 and later, the movement of many of these men and women to America, and especially New York, intensified the determination of anthropologists and other scholars to launch a scholarly counterattack against the racist propaganda of the fascists.

One result of this counterattack was that by the 1940s the idea of "race" had become in many quarters a sort of taboo. Scholars in

general and social scientists in particular preferred to talk about
"minority groups," and for some even the concept of "ethnic
group" was suspect. In an analogous manner, what had formerly
been called "race relations" was referred to as "intergroup
relations." It could be argued that from a sociological point of
view, the coining of such neologisms was a form of know-nothingism.
In some cases it was based on the well-intentioned but naive
premise that if you do not talk about something it will go away.

It appears that it was only in the 1950s that some sociologists
regained enough confidence in their own perspective to reassert
that racial groups are "real" when they are so defined by people in
society. During the 1940s, however, the sociologists were not
prepared to bring embarrassing questions which seemed to imply
that racial conflict was not simply a product of irrational and
pathological factors. Sociologists, along with psychologists and
social psychologists, tended to devote their energies to schemes for
the reduction of intergroup conflict. The perspective of Robert
Park, who believed in the persistence of conflict between races and
ethnic groups, was apparently too pessimistic to be popular in the
hopeful mood of the 1940s and 1950s.[1]

This generalization is supported by an examination of what was
the most important study in the 1940s of the Negro in America, *An
American Dilemma*. Gunnar Myrdal's study contained a rationale
for the activist and optimistic ideology which appealed to most
American social scientists interested in race relations after the war.
Significantly, Myrdal included in that study an explicit attack upon
what he called the "overly pessimistic" race relations theory of
Robert Park.

The Myrdal study reflected the concern and anxiety felt by many
Americans with "Negro morale" during the war. It was apparent
that black Americans were growing increasingly restive as they were
denied an equal opportunity for employment in war industries and
faced continued discrimination in the armed forces, housing, and
other sectors of life. The concern with morale among Negroes was
intensified when racial riots broke out in cities such as Detroit and
in Harlem. Despite these factors, Myrdal ignored Negro protest
and racial consciousness. He preferred to look at the problem of
race relations as a problem of individual pathology and irrationality.
His avoidance of the question of group consciousness and its

advantages is in some respects analogous to that of social scientists in the 1920s and 1930s.

An American Dilemma was published in 1944 under the auspices of the Carnegie Corporation. As Myrdal pointed out in the preface, the study had an unusual character in that it was not a product of an academic institution but was sponsored by a philanthropic organization and "in a sense, carried out within the corporation." Myrdal claimed that he was an objective scholar, not because he had thought through the Negro problem in the United States or had any training or expertise in race relations research, but because he "previously had given hardly a thought" to the problem and "was nearly stripped of all the familiar and conventinal moorings of viewpoints and valuations."[2]

In retrospect this latter disclaimer of Myrdal's appears rather disingenuous, for the most popular criticism of *An American Dilemma* was that it was overly optimistic. Myrdal's major thesis was that the Negro problem was one of ideology or irrational psychology. His optimism with regard to the future of American race relations was based upon his belief that white Americans would not desire to remain inconsistent and ambivalent. White Americans felt a dissonance between their democratic ideals and their treatment of Negroes, a dissonance which they would attempt to alleviate, because it caused psychic discomfort.

Despite Myrdal's assertion that he was free of values, or what he called valuations, it is apparent that one purpose of his book was to create a new orientation for American society and its social scientists; thus it had an ideological purpose. Myrdal repeatedly claimed that the prevailing point of view among American race relations scholars was pessimistic. This pessimism was rooted in a belief that race relations were an outgrowth of competitive strivings among races within the industrial order. As we shall see below, Myrdal attempted to denigrate this theory as a product of an outmoded conservatism associated with Herbert Spencer and William Graham Sumner, symbolic *bêtes noires* of American liberals. As suggested above, Myrdal favored the view that the race relations problem was a psychological one. Whenever Myrdal came across evidence of Negro frustration or despair over the handicaps they faced in educational or economic competition, he sidestepped the question of competition. In general, he asserted, pessimism was not really American, for the key element in the American psyche was optimism and a faith in democratic ideals.

Myrdal was opposed to what he called the "do-nothing" sociology of William Graham Sumner, because he believed that it led to a "fatalistic" attitude toward changing racial mores in the American South. Myrdal assumed that Sumner remained a social Darwinist and that his concepts of folkways and mores were connected with and tainted by his laissez-faire ideology. Myrdal was aware that the sociologists trained under Robert Park and others at the University of Chicago had approached the social behavior of whites and blacks in the South as a question of slowly changing mores. These mores served to alleviate status anxieties by giving people who were formerly slaves a definite place and code of behavior etiquette.[3]

This orientation had led the Chicago sociologists to view racial etiquette and the segregated society it underlay as only slowly changing. It is important to note how this orientation clashed with that of Myrdal. According to the Chicago viewpoint, older people in the South, white and black, were adapted to these behavior patterns and were uncomfortable when they were broken or when they traveled to the North where racial patterns remained more fluid and chaotic. Younger Negroes, although there were regional and class differences, were tending to chip away at the system of etiquette. Yet there was a great deal of frustration and disorganization among American Negroes, especially those who believed in the promise of greater opportunity. The younger Negroes were becoming more disillusioned, although the entire group seemed to be losing its faith in America.[4]

Myrdal thought the emphasis the Chicago school placed upon slowly evolving mores and race conflict in a competitive society threatened his own theory. The latter was based upon the assumption that people felt a great discomfort because of their undemocratic treatment and prejudicial attitudes toward blacks. The Chicago orientation suggested, however, that many people were most comfortable when the Negro stayed in his "place." At the same time, Myrdal believed that the industrial system was a rationalizing force and that as the South became industrialized whites would become more liberal and "rational" in their attitudes toward Negroes. For Myrdal, race conflict was grounded in the ignorance of whites who were finally becoming aware of "the tremendous social costs of keeping up the present irrational and illegal caste system." The Chicago view of race relations, on the contrary, was that group conflict was a natural product of competition for jobs, space, and status.[5]

The attack Myrdal made upon the Chicago orientation and the ideas of Robert Park can be traced to the fact that the Chicago view of race relations was in competition with that of Myrdal. Although Myrdal did not directly attack Park for his conflict perspective, he did attempt to link Park and his students to William Graham Sumner, because they both used the concept of mores. The idea of slowly evolving mores was one which Myrdal had to attack, because it seemed to be connected with the old idea that legislation had to follow mores.

Myrdal believed that what he called Sumner's do-nothing attitudes were exemplified in the following passage from the latter's *Folkways* of 1906:

The combination in the mores of persistency and variability determines the extent to which it is possible to modify them by arbitrary action. It is not possible to change them, by any artifice or device, to a great extent, or suddenly, or in any essential element; it is possible to modify them by slow and long-continued effort if the ritual is changed by minute variations.[6]

According to Myrdal such pronouncements indicated that Sumner's theory was nothing more than a "reformulation and slight modification of the old laissez-faire doctrine of the natural order . . . human relations are governed by 'natural laws.' " This is a rather distorted reading of Sumner, who appeared to be stating that it was hard to change old and embedded habits and that men are governed by customs which are not changed suddenly.

At the same time it should be noted that Robert Park and his students did not claim that Southern racial etiquette and customs were not changing. On the contrary, they drew a distinction between those regions where customs were breaking down and those which were more isolated and where the behavior system based upon the plantation system still prevailed.

It is doubtful whether a closer and more sympathetic reading of some of the Chicago sociologists would have altered Myrdal's views in any fundamental manner. Myrdal found the concept of mores distasteful, not only because it led to "conservative" attitudes toward the efficacy of legislation in the area of race relations, but also because it was based upon the idea that customs were not rational. Myrdal asserted repeatedly that Americans wanted to be rational as well as to act consistently. The concept of mores suggested that people acted irrationally (in the sense of an unquestioning acceptance) much of the time. People were likely to prefer to be comfortable or even conformist in most areas of their lives. It is perhaps significant in this regard that Myrdal's study does not delve into the psychological irrationalities which were emphasized by Freudians and neo-Freudians in their explorations of race relations. Some Chicago sociologists, including Charles S. Johnson and E. Franklin Frazier, were attempting to use the ideas of neo-Freudians like Harry Stack Sullivan in their works. It is interesting to note that Robert Park, in a letter to Myrdal in 1939, suggested that Myrdal or anyone who was undertaking a study of race relations in America needed to comprehend the psychoanalytic approaches to prejudice and to the peculiar situation of the Negro in American life.[7]

Park's letter to Myrdal revealed that Park had retained his concern with the group consciousness of blacks in America. He felt that with the general loss of religious faith among Negroes there was a "loss of consolation" and that Negroes in general were in need of "some sort of moral discipline." Although there was some indication, in Park's view, of an intensified race consciousness among Negroes, it did not appear that discontent was much reduced. In fact, restlessness and anxiety had been increasing among all classes of Negroes in recent years.[8]

Park's letter to Myrdal revealed that Park was growing somewhat more pessimistic about the chances for Negroes to achieve a moral solidarity within the United States. This pessimism was amplified in an article on "Racial Ideologies" which Park contributed to a volume entitled *American Society in Wartime*. In that article, published in 1943, Park adopted an approach which clashed markedly with that of Myrdal. The racial doctrines which Americans associate with the South, Park suggested, were not localized in that region. Rather, the racial attitudes of Americans in the North, South, East, and West were fundamentally the same, differing only in emphasis and detail.

Park believed that "back of these racial doctrines is the whole history of the South and of the United States." It was impossible to understand those doctrines without becoming acquainted in an intimate fashion with the people "in whose minds they grew up. For racial ideologies are no mere logical artifacts, formulas, or general conception; they are rather the historical products of long-continued conflict and controversy."[9]

Park differed from Myrdal not only because he held the view that racial ideologies were products of both historical and contemporary conflicts and were thus embedded in peoples' consciousness, but also in his belief that America was not an idealistic or especially moral nation. One of Myrdal's basis assumptions was that America was a "moralistic and moral-conscious" nation and that the individual American was the "opposite of a cynic." His study, Myrdal felt, offered a "hope for great improvement in the near future" and accounted for "the dominant role of ideals in the social dynamics of America." Park, on the other hand, claimed that despite superficial alterations in the attitudes of some Americans toward Negroes during the Second World War, most Americans remained highly race conscious. In his article of 1943, Park's last work on race relations, he made the same basic argument that he had made in his first article in 1913. Americans still saw the Negro as a symbol and not as an individualized person. He claimed that:

There are still relatively few people in the United States who are able, even if they wished to do so, to treat a Negro democratically, that is, on his merits as an individual rather than as a representative of his race. . . . [I]t is just here that the racial policy of the United States is identical with that of Australia and South Africa, whose racial ideologies must be reckoned with in winning the war and making the peace.[10]

Park felt that the United Nations could not "win the peace" unless its constituent nations achieved a fundamental and even revolutionary alteration in their attitudes toward colored and colonial peoples. Yet, he argued, for all their apparent success in the development of techniques for measuring opinion and in improving or undermining public morale, political scientists and propaganda experts had not discovered any techniques for bringing about significant changes in the public mind. Park expected that both in America and throughout the world peoples and races would continue to struggle for the political and racial equality which had been denied them "in the world that was passing." Since Park did not expect that scientific or social scientific expertise would play much of a role in resolving those conflicts, it is understandable that men like Gunnar Myrdal would read Park's work as a counsel of despair.[11]

As his life drew to a close, Park began to articulate his vision of the cultural crisis which had enveloped Europe and America. The Second World War in his lifetime seemed to focus his attention upon that crisis, which he had first sensed in America in the 1920s. Some scholars have asserted that Robert Park, along with several other American intellectuals, was involved in a rather naive and "romantic" quest for a lost social order and a quest for community. Park's last works reveal, however, that his vision of modern civilization was more sophisticated than his critics have acknowledged it to have been.[12]

In the last article published in his lifetime, in 1944, entitled "Missions and the Modern World," Park claimed that the Great Society of Europe and the United States was threatened by the centrifugal forces of class, race, and religion, forces which men could not control and which its experts and professionals did not seem to understand. That Great Society was suffering from inner strains which resulted from its size and impersonal power. Park argued that:

In America the racial and class feeling of the new immigrants shows itself unexpectedly resistant to the dissolving force of national consciousness. In England the "particularism" of trades and professions and the racial feeling of Wales or Ulster, of Scotland or Catholic Ireland, seem to be growing stronger and not weaker.

More threatening still to the cohesion of the Great Society are the motives openly avowed by some of the American and European masters of concentrated capital—the men who direct enormous social power without attempting to form a social purpose, who smash working-class unions with no idea of any system to take their place, who boast that their trade is their politics and corrupt whole parties merely to increase the personal wealth which they will waste in making or buying things they hardly desire. The "cash nexus" has, no more than the "voting nexus," insured that common membership of the Great Society shall mean a common interest in its solidarity.[13]

Park went on to argue that technological "advances" such as transportation systems and communications networks, like the political apparatus of laws and treaties and elections, were merely "mechanical arrangements" which could not lead to either national or international solidarity. His conversations with citizens of modern cities led him to conclude that they but dimly recognized the greater society and, if they thought of it at all, often thought of it merely with distrust and dislike.

The politics and literature of the twentieth century, in Park's view, was a continuing commentary on and expression of a conscious or semi-conscious fear of the dissolution of society and civilization. Men were anxious lest the civilization of the Great Society "which we have adopted so rapidly and with so little forethought may prove unable to secure either a harmonious life for its members or even its own stability." Park sensed that there was not room left for "the old delight" in manifest destiny or "the tide of progress" and claimed that even the newer belief in an "effortless evolution" of social institutions was gone. In a striking commentary on his own generation, he asserted that it was unable to provide the direction needed in a period of crisis, for its intellectual habits ran toward specialization. He argued that it was necessary to recognize that "a society whose intellectual direction consisted only of unrelated specialisms must drift and that we dare drift no longer."[14]

In the articles published in the two years before he died, Park appears to have lost the confidence which he had once possessed in the intricate webbing of social and economic life and the cohesive force of competition and conflict. In his view America lacked a common culture and intellectual direction and, like Western Civilization as a whole, remained precariously balanced between the forces of cohesion and dissolution. Yet, in an interesting article, "Education and the Cultural Crisis," published in 1943, Park suggested that perhaps the crucible of a new civilization and a "new indigenous race" was developing in the state of California. Despite what he recognized as its footloose and dispossessed proletariat and its provision of a rich soil for "a wild, weedy growth of political isms and religious cults," California represented an environment where the diverse races and cultures of America were meeting and intermixing. That state's congeries of culturally insulated communities, Park felt, suggested that the United States had already "measureably achieved the communistic ideal of a classless society —that is, a society without any hierarchical structure or, one might almost say, a society with no structure at all."[15]

It may seem as if Park's tentative formulation of California's significance for America's and the world's future was merely a refusal on his part to submit to the pessimistic conclusions which apparently followed from his analysis of modern civilization and its crisis. Park, however, did not relish the role of Cassandra and his criticism of modern culture was more complex and subtle than that of most American intellectuals. Although he recognized the centrifugal forces in social and economic life, he seems to have drawn upon his own version of a frontier theory to sustain his hopes in the future of democracy. For Park, California was a symbol of the "last frontier," a region and an environment where races and peoples would intermix and intermingle. His theory of a democratic frontier might bear only a resemblance to that of Frederick Jackson Turner and other scholars and intellectuals, but it served Park, like others, as a source of hope.

Yet Park knew that when social and economic changes were great and communities were weakened and even shattered by accelerated migration, what he called the "intricate web of normal expectation" was torn into bits. His knowledge of this disruptive process, however, remained in a dynamic tension with his belief in the creation of something new and undetermined where cultural and racial frontiers existed. But would cultural intermixture lead to cultural fusion and the solidarity that such fusion implies? Did California represent a new start or was it merely a magnetic field which attracted the loose components of American society? Park did not answer these questions, but, in any case, it was clear that his vision of America's dilemma was distinct and perhaps deeper than that of Gunnar Myrdal. Park could not share in Myrdal's optimistic ideology or believe in the latter's vision of the American dilemma and its resolution.

NOTES

1. Herbert Blumer, "Reflections on the Theory of Race Relations," in Andrew W. Lind (ed.), *Race Relations in World Perspective* (Honolulu, 1955), pp. 3-5.

2. Gunnar Myrdal, *An American Dilemma* (New York, 1944), pp. lix-lxi.

3. Ibid., pp. 1031-32; Robert Park, "Introduction" to Bertram W. Boyle, *The Etiquette of Race Relations in the South* (Chicago, 1937), reprinted in Park, *Race and Culture* (New York, 1964), pp. 177-88.

4. Charles S. Johnson, *Shadow of the Plantation* (Chicago, 1934), and idem, *Growing Up in the Black Belt* (Washington, D.C., 1941); E. Franklin Frazier, *Negro Youth at the Crossways* (Washington, D.C., 1941).

5. Myrdal, *An American Dilemma*, p. 1009.

6. Ibid., pp. 1048-57.

7. Harry Stack Sullivan had been informally connected with the Chicago sociologists since the late 1920s. He was a consultant to both Charles S. Johnson and E. Franklin Frazier when they were working on their book on Negro Youth for the American Council of Education (see note 4 above). Myrdal did seem to be impressed by one writer, John Dollard, who worked with psychoanalytical concepts. See Myrdal, ibid., p. 1202.

8. Robert Park to Gunnar Myrdal, February 14, 1939, Nashville, Tennessee (Box 1, Folder 12, Robert Park Papers, Fisk University).

9. Robert Park, "Racial Ideologies," in William F. Ogburn (ed.), *American Society in Wartime* (Chicago, 1943), pp. 165-83, reprinted in idem, *Race and Culture*, pp. 310-11.

10. Ibid., p. 314; Myrdal, *An American Dilemma*, pp. lxx, lxi.

11. For an indication that Park's students did not share his ideas regarding the the role of social scientists in the resolution of conflict, see Louis Wirth, "Research in Racial and Cultural Relations," *Midwest Journal*, 1 (1948-50), 18. See also Kurt Lewin, in Gertrude Weiss Lewin (ed.), *Resolving Social Conflicts: Selected Papers on Group Dynamics, 1935-1946* (New York, 1943).

12. Morton and Lucia White, *The Intellectual Versus the City* (Cambridge, Mass., 1962). An interesting criticism of this book and other works on the quest for community is contained in Park Dixon Goist, "City and 'Community': The Urban Theory of Robert Park," *American Quarterly*, XXIII (1971), 46-47, 54-56. On the relation of Park and other American sociologists to "conservative" and "pessimistic" ideas developed in Europe and transmitted to America, see Leon Bramson, *the Political Context of Sociology* (Princeton, N.J., 1961).

13. Robert Park, "Missions and the Modern World," *American Journal of Sociology*, L (1944), 177-83, reprinted in idem, *Race and Culture*, pp. 336-37.

14. Ibid., p. 338.

15. Robert Park, "Education and the Cultural Crisis," *American Journal of Sociology*, LXVIII (1943), 728-36, reprinted in idem, *Race and Culture*, pp. 316-20, 324.

EPILOGUE

In a recent article Edward Shils has argued that Robert Park's thought was incoherent and, by implication, less mature than more systematic social theorists such as Talcott Parsons. This study has taken the opposite tack, stressing the continuity of Park's thought over several decades as well as its continued vitality. Park, like another protean social theorist located at the University of Chicago, George Herbert Mead, did not complete a sustained theoretical work during his lifetime. Park's articles were collected by those who sought to perpetuate his intellectual heritage around 1950. From Park's retirement in the mid-1930s until the mid-1950s and perhaps later, this heritage was shaped in large part by the "oral tradition" at Chicago and within the sociological profession.[1]

The study was undertaken in the first place due to the fact that I was both disturbed and puzzled. As a historian involved in teaching sociology with a particular interest in what we term race and ethnicity, I was bothered by how little the Thomas-Park perspective was used or respected by contemporary theorists. As a teacher and student of sociological theory and methods, I was puzzled by the obvious disjunction of generations, by what some term the "decline" of the Chicago school.

The entire concept of a Chicago "school," I would discover, was problematic. Many of the most productive and active theorists and researchers who were affiliated with Chicago shunned the concept of school as if it connoted some rigid and blind following of tradition. Yet there was a deep sense of tradition and pride at or immediately beneath the surface of their discourse as professionals and as persons. Perhaps this apparent ambivalence and lack of clarity of perspective is indicative of much sociological thought. There are traditions in sociology, but there are few systems of thought and sentiment which approximate what Thomas Kuhn has termed paradigms.

A paradigm and works so impressive and programmatic that they deserve the term "exemplar," Kuhn has argued, are the primary shaping perspectives of a unit of study, a discipline or specialization. If a paradigm is present and scholars of talent have created exemplary studies, the problems of the discipline are clearly formulated and ready to be penetrated and elaborated. As I read the work of Thomas and Park and some of their students such as E. Franklin Frazier, Louis Wirth, and E. C. Hughes, it appeared that both a paradigm and exemplary works in the area of race and ethnicity were present. Yet the works of contemporary sociological theorists and researchers seldom referred to these earlier figures. Moreover, the reputation of central figures such as Park were under great attack on what increasingly struck me as flimsy grounds whether the grounds were based upon scientific, policy, or moral assumptions.

Had Park's works been reissued during the racial and ethnic conflict of the 1960s, they might have had a greater impact and received more attention. The 1950s and early 1960s, however, were not a fertile period for the sort of ideas and values underlying Park's work. Yet by the 1970s the international and comparative thrust of the Thomas-Park perspective on race and ethnic relations began to appeal to scholars once again. The rather smug and parochial attitudes shaping social science, sometimes termed the "consensus" view in historical studies, were shattered. Several historians have taken up themes at the center of Thomas and Park's work.[2] Several British scholars, working in the midst of an ethnic and racial turmoil analogous to that which animated Park and Thomas in the 1910s, have also noted the relevance of this tradition of theory and research.[3]

A few American sociologists have taken up comparative ethnicity as a central topic. Among the most ambitious of these are the works of R. A. Schermerhorn, E. K. Francis, P. van den Berghe, Stephen Steinberg, and the economist Thomas Sowell.[4] Yet despite these stirrings of interest I doubt that the approach pioneered at Chicago, especially in its comparative thrust, will become popular in American sociology. The reasons for this judgment are many, but the major determinants deserve some summary.

At the level of method and procedure, the program of Thomas and Park was rooted in an empathetic view of the social psychology of groups and peoples previously or currently subordinated. During the period when American sociologists were less obsessed with methodological questions, the looser and more open-ended "field" observations of a Park or Thomas were legitimate. This tradition, more anthropological and historical than those fashionable after the 1930s, rested on a belief or presupposition about the power and validity of sophisticated observation. This observation was to be guided by what Herbert Blumer later termed "sensitizing concepts." These observations, stimulated and/or checked by the use of literary works, autobiographies, life histories, and interviews, seemed too "unscientific" to later generations of sociologists. What was seen by many as a methodological looseness and mere description lost favor in the early 1930s as more "positivist" orientations toward the collection and analysis of data took hold.[5]

Recent work in the history of social science suggests that Park, contrary to a common stereotype, was not antiquantitative or antistatistical. If his own talents and predelictions lay in the direction of an empathetic uncovering of attitudes and movements of thought, he was if anything a methodological pluralist. The method of investigation, for Park and for most Chicago figures, should be consonant with the phenomena to be investigated. Certainly the favored methods of Park, as exemplified in some detail in works such as "Methods of a Race Survey" of 1926, raised difficult problems. Yet, in retrospect, Park's suggested procedures were no more or less "scientific" than the more narrowly conceived and often ahistorical studies of attitudes which were so popular during the next decades.[6]

At the level of theory rather than method, there were two major characteristics of Park's general point of view which made the transmission of his approach problematical. Park's work, especially in the area of race and ethnic studies, reflected a cosmopolitan and detached attitude that was lost as American social scientists in general (cultural anthropologists being the noteworthy exception) and sociologists in particular grew more parochial. Students were much more likely to be trained in statistics rather than the languages which would open up non-English groups to investigation.

The study of race and ethnicity became more closely tied to social work and education under the rubric of "intergroup" or "human" relations. Several of Park's students remarked upon this movement toward ethnocentrism and what they saw as an emphasis upon a social problems approach to issues of race and ethnicity.[7]

A second characteristic of Park's work was, as developed in earlier portions of this study, his "conflict" approach. It is not especially important to trace the filiation of Park's basic "realism" or "pessimism" to a Darwinian world view or to particular scholars such as Gumplowitz, Sumner, or Small. Park drew upon a number of thinkers and selected important portions of their works for his (and Ernest Burgess's) *Introduction to the Science of Society* of 1921. From a variety of scholars and, equally important, from his own experience and travel through the American South, Europe, and immigrant neighborhoods, Park achieved his sophisticated and rounded view of the origin and persistence of "ethnicity." From all accounts Park and Thomas were both voracious readers and voracious observers of social life. From this point of view, it is not surprising that no figure with their scope and comparative-historical expertise arrived at Chicago or elsewhere to perpetuate, let alone to elaborate their heritage.[8]

If a single figure was ready both to sustain Park's program and to elaborate it in a critical fashion it was the black sociologist E. Franklin Frazier. It was a tragedy that this ambitious and talented theorist and researcher never received a call to the university where he received his doctorate. Frazier was undoubtedly embittered by the fact that, despite several honors late in his career, he never had the graduate students or financial apparatus for research and graduate training available at universities like Chicago.[9]

The field of race and ethnic relations suffered greatly from the failure of American sociologists to take up, criticize, and elaborate the ideas and concepts of Robert Park and W. I. Thomas. As suggested in the preceding chapter Gunnar Myrdal's general approach, certainly no more "testable" or heuristic than Park's, was better attuned to a broad consensus which emphasized the power of liberal ideas in a democratic society and correspondingly de-emphasized sources of ethnic and racial tension.

It is clear from our contemporary vantage point that this liberal consensus came to a bitter and confusing end after the urban, racial, ethnic and generational conflicts of the 1960s and early

1970s. American social scientists along with those from Europe and elsewhere in the world now appear to be reconstructing theoretical and methodological approaches to recurrent "ethnicity" and "ethnogenesis." If these approaches are to be of more value, in scientific, public policy, or human terms than those of the post-Myrdal era, I suspect they will eventually come to terms with the comparative-historical and "realistic" approaches pioneered by Park, Thomas, and their most creative students of society.

NOTES

1. Edward Shils, "Some Academics, Mainly in Chicago," *American Scholar*, 50 (1981), 188-90. Cf. the general analysis of Chicago sociology in his *The Present State of American Sociology* (Glencoe, Ill., 1948). On the transmission of ideas and concepts at Chicago, see Paul Rock, *The Making of Symbolic Interactionism* (London, 1979).

2. John Higham, *Send These to Me: Jews and Other Immigrants in Urban America* (New York, 1975), pp. 231-46. The early work of Oscar Handlin was influenced by Chicago sociology. See especially the comprehensive discussion in Maldwyn A. Jones, "Oscar Handlin," in Marcus Cunliffe and Robin Winks (eds.), *Pastmasters: Some Essays on American Historians* (New York, 1969), pp. 239-77. A recent valuable study which takes up several questions posed by Park is George M. Fredrickson's *White Supremacy: A Comparative Study in American and South African History* (New York, 1981). The most comprehensive comparative sociology by a figure working in the Thomas-Park tradition is Morris Janowitz, *The Last Half-Century: Societal Change and Politics in America* (Chicago, 1978).

3. Michael Banton, "1960: A Turning Point in the Study of Race Relations," in Sidney W. Mintz (ed.), *Slavery, Colonialism, and Racism* (New York, 1974), 131-44; Martin Bulmer, "Charles S. Johnson, Robert E. Park and the research methods of the Chicago Commission on Race Relations, 1919-22: an early experiment in applied social research," *Ethnic and Racial Studies*, 4 (1981), 289-306.

4. R. A. Schermerhorn, *Comparative Ethnic Relations: A Framework for Theory and Research* (New York, 1975, 1981); E. K. Francis, *Ethnic Relations* (New York, 1975); P. van den Berghe, *The Ethnic Phenomenon* (New York, 1981); Stephen Steinberg, *The Ethnic Myth: Race, Ethnicity, and Class in America* (New York, 1981); and Thomas Sowell, *Ethnic Groups in America* (Cambridge, Mass., 1980). Cf. the essays in Jan Berting, Felix Geyer, and Ray Jurkovich (eds.), *Problems in International Comparative Research in the Social Science* (Oxford, 1979), especially John Rex, "Race Relations Theory and the Study of Migration to Ad-

vanced Industrial Societies," and P. van den Berghe, "The Present State of Comparative Race and Ethnic Studies."

5. There is no satisfactory account of the drive for methodological sophistication and even purity in American sociology. A promising essay on the shift from "soft" to "hard" methods is Norbert Wiley's "The Rise and Fall of Dominating Theories in American Sociology," in William E. Snizek, Ellsworth R. Fuhrman, and Michael K. Miller (eds.), *Contemporary Issues in Theory and Research: A Metasociological Perspective* (Westport, Conn., 1979), pp. 48-57. See also Fred H. Matthews, *Quest for an American Sociology: Robert E. Park and the Chicago School* (Montreal, 1977), pp. 179-85.

6. Martin Bulmer, "Quantification and Chicago Social Science in the 1920s: A Neglected Tradition," *Journal of the History of the Behavioral Sciences*, 17 (1981), 312-31.

7. Herbert Blumer, "Research on Race Relations: United States of America," *International Bulletin of Social Science*, 10 (1958), 403-47; Everett C. Hughes, "Race Relations and the Sociological Imagination," *American Sociological Review*, 28 (1963), and idem, "Ethnocentric Sociology," *Social Forces*, 40 (1961), both reprinted in *The Sociological Eye* (Chicago, 1971).

8. Edward Shils, note 1 above, and idem, "Tradition, Ecology, and Institution in the History of Sociology," in idem., *The Calling of Sociology and Other Essays on the Pursuit of Learning* (Chicago, 1980), pp. 185-88, 218, 239-40. The difficulties inherent in the perpetuation and elaboration of research traditions in sociology are treated in Edward A. Tiryakian, "The Significance of Schools in the Development of Sociology," in Snizek, Fuhrman, and Miller, *Contemporary Issues*.

9. G. Franklin Edwards, "E. Franklin Frazier," in James E. Blackwell and Morris Janowitz (eds.), *Black Sociologists: Historical and Contemporary Perspectives* (Chicago, 1974), and G. Franklin Edwards (ed.), *E. Franklin Frazier on Race Relations* (Chicago, 1968), "Introduction" and especially Chaps. 1-7. Louis W. Cosey, "E. Franklin Frazier's Analysis of the Problems of the Negro" (unpublished M.A. thesis, University of Southern California, 1957).

BIBLIOGRAPHICAL ESSAY

Most of the sources for this study are referred to in the footnotes. The most valuable unpublished documents are housed in the Archives of the Regenstein Library at the University of Chicago. The Park Papers are especially rich for the period up to 1930 and may be supplemented for later years by the small collection at Fisk University, Nashville, Tennessee. The Booker T. Washington Papers at the Library of Congress, Washington, D.C., contain material relating to Park's participation in the "Tuskegee Machine." Other collections at the Regenstein include the papers of Ernest Burgess, Louis Wirth, and Robert Redfield.

By far the most stimulating book on Chicago sociology is Fred H. Matthews's *Quest for an American Sociology: Robert E. Park and the Chicago School* (Montreal, McGill-Queen's University Press, 1977), which is available in paperback. Matthews careful and largely sympathetic study may be supplemented by the uncritical biography by Park's student of the 1920s, Winifred Rauschenbush, *Robert E. Park: Biography of a Sociologist* (Durham, N.C., Duke University Press, 1979). There is no biography of W. I. Thomas, but Evan Thomas of the University of Iowa is working on an intellectual biography.

On the University of Chicago environment see Richard J. Storr, *Harper's University: The Beginnings* (Chicago, University of Chicago Press, 1966), and James Carey, *Sociology and Public Affairs: The Chicago School* (Beverly Hills, Calif., Sage Publications, 1975). Carey has deposited several interesting interviews with Chicago students of the 1920s in the Regenstein library. Robert E. L. Faris has collected information on the Chicago department in the 1920s in his *Chicago Sociology, 1920-1932* (San Francisco, Chandler, 1967) and has included an appendix which contains a list of M.A. and Ph.D. students from the 1890s through 1932.

The theoretical critique of the 1930s is largely summarized in two volumes—Milla A. Alihan's *Social Ecology: A Critical Analysis* (New York, Columbia University Press, 1938) and Herbert Blumer's *An Appraisal of Thomas and Znaniecki's The Polish Peasant in Europe and America* (New York, Social Science Research Council, 1939). In 1947, Blumer's "in-house" critique was expanded by Edward Shils in his *The Present State of American Sociology* (Glencoe, Ill., Free Press, 1948). Those seriously concerned with Park's style of thought will benefit from the recent translations of the works of Georg Simmel and the recent study of a chief translator, David Frisby's *A Reassessment of Georg Simmel's Social Theory* (London, Heinemann, 1981).

A stimulating work on Chicago theory especially helpful for understanding the difficulties of transmitting concepts is Paul Rock, *The Making of Symbolic Interactionism* (London, Macmillan, 1979). See also Martin Bulmer's extensive article "The Early Institutionalization of Social Science Resarch: The Local Community Research Committee at the University of Chicago 1923-30," in *Minerva*, 18 (1980).

Valuable portrayals of early work in race and ethnic studies are contained in Maurice Stein's *The Eclipse of Community, An Interpretation of American Studies* (Princeton, N.J., Princeton University Press, 1960), and Peter Rose's *The Subject Is Race: Traditional Ideologies and the Teaching of Race Relations* (New York, Oxford University Press, 1968). Rose's *They and We, Racial and Ethnic Relations in the United States*, 3rd edition (New York, Random House, 1981) is the best short introduction to the subject. Joseph Hraba's *American Ethnicity* (Itasca, Ill., F. E. Peacock, 1979) is also impressive. Howard Odum's neglected *American Sociology, The Story of Sociology in the United States through 1950* (New York, Longmans, Green and Co., 1951) contains a great deal of important autobiographical data.

Among the few Chicago sociologists who have written on their own heritage is Everett C. Hughes. His essays on Chicago can be found in *The Sociological Eye* (Chicago, Aldine, 1971). Hughes and his wife Helen MacGill Hughes wrote a book which was consciously in the Park mode, *Where Peoples Meet, Racial and Ethnic Frontiers* (Glencoe, Ill., Free Press, 1952). E. C. Hughes also edited, with Edgar T. Thompson, an interesting reader on *Race: Individual and Collective Behavior* (New York, Free Press, 1958).

Several Chicago figures have been included as subjects in the University of Chicago Press's series titled "The Heritage of Sociology." Among the strongest volumes containing the most insightful introductions are the following—Morris Janowitz (ed.), *W. I. Thomas on Social Organization and Social Personality* (1966); Anselm Strauss (ed.), *George Herbert Mead on Social Psychology* (1964); James Short, Jr. (ed.), *The Social Fabric of the Metropolis: Contribution of the Chicago School of Urban Sociology*

(1971); and Robert Bierstedt (ed.), *Florian Znaniecki on Humanistic Sociology* (1969). No volume has as yet appeared on Ellsworth Faris, long the chairman of the department. Information on Faris can be found in J. David Lewis and Richard L. Smith, *American Sociology and Pragmatism: Mead, Chicago Sociology, and Symbolic Interaction* (Chicago, University of Chicago Press, 1980), but the book as a whole falls short of what its title promises.

There is little material on black sociologists available, although work is proceeding in many places. The best short introduction is John H. Bracy, Jr., August Meier, and Elliott Rudwick (eds.), *The Black Sociologists: The First Half Century* (Belmont, Calif., Wadsworth, 1971), which is a book of primary sources. The essays collected in James Blackwell and Morris Janowitz (eds.), *Black Sociologists* (Chicago, University of Chicago Press, 1974), are uneven in quality, although those on Charles S. Johnson and E. Franklin Frazier are still worth reviewing. Although his anti black nationalist bias skews some of his interpretations, S. P. Fullinwider's *The Mind and Mood of Black America: 20th Century Thought* (Homewood, Ill., Dorsey, 1969) is among the most sustained examinations of black intellectuals. See also, on black thinkers in general, James O. Young, *Black Writers of the Thirties* (Baton Rouge, La., Louisiana State University Press, 1973), and John B. Kirby, *Black Americans in the Roosevelt Era: Liberalism and Race* (Knoxville, Tenn., University of Tennessee Press, 1980).

By the mid-1960s, many black intellectuals had grown very critical of sociology. Although earlier figures had seen it as a destroyer of stereotypes these critics saw it as sustaining a warped and less-than-human image of black Americans. This is especially true of the work of Ralph Ellison's *Shadow and Act* (New York, Random, 1964) and Albert Murray's *The Omni-Americans* (New York, Outerbridge and Dienstfrey, 1970). An interesting collection which is revealing of the late-1960s climate of opinion is Ann J. Lane (ed.), *The Debate over Slavery: Stanley Elkins and His Critics* (Urbana, Ill., University of Illinois Press, 1971). Although Harold Cruse's *The Crisis of the Negro Intellectual* (New York, William Morrow, 1967) does not focus on white academics, its scope and polemical power make it still worth examining. Last, but far from least, see the powerful and subtle autobiography by Horace Cayton, *Long Old Road* (New York, Trident, 1965). Cayton was trained at Chicago but eschewed an academic career and co-authored the matchless *Black Metropolis* with the anthropologist St. Clair Drake.

SELECTED BIBLIOGRAPHY

BOOKS

Abbott, Edith (ed.). *Historical Aspects of the Immigration Problem.* Chicago: University of Chicago Press, 1926.

Adamic, Louis. *A Nation of Nations.* New York: Harper and Brothers, 1945.

Adams, Romanzo. *Interracial Marriage in Hawaii.* New York: Macmillan, 1937.

Baker, Ray S. *Following the Color Line.* New York: Neale, 1914.

Berkson, Isaac B. *Theories of Americanization, A Critical Study With Special Reference to the Jewish Group.* New York: Columbia University Press, 1920.

Boas, Franz. *The Mind of Primitive Man.* New York: Macmillan; revised edition, New York: Free Press, 1965.

_____. *Race and Democratic Society.* New York: J. J. Augustin, 1945.

Bogardus, Emory S. *Immigration and Race Attitudes.* Boston: D. C. Heath, 1928.

_____. *Essentials of Americanization.* Los Angeles: University of Southern California Press, 1923.

Bourne, Randolph. *The History of a Literary Radical and Other Papers.* New York: B. W. Huebsch, 1920.

The Chicago Commission on Race Relations. *The Negro in Chicago.* Chicago: University of Chicago Press, 1922.

Commons, John R. *Races and Immigrants in America.* New York: Macmillan, 1920.

Dollard, John. *Caste and Class in a Southern Town.* New Haven: Yale University Press, 1937.

Dowd, Jerome. *The Negro in American Life*. New York: Century, 1926.

Drachsler, Julius. *Democracy and Assimilation: the Building of Immigrant Heritages in America*. New York: Macmillan, 1920.

Drake, St. Clair, and Cayton, Horace R. *Black Metropolis, A Study of Negro Life in a Northern City*. New York: Harcourt, Brace, 1945.

Du Bois, W.E.B. *Dusk of Dawn: An Essay Toward the Autobiography of a Race Concept*. New York: Harcourt, Brace, 1940.

_____. *The Souls of Black Folk: Essays and Sketches*. Chicago: A. C. McClurg, 1931.

Duncan, Hannibal G. *Immigration and Assimilation*. Boston: D. C. Heath, 1933.

Embree, Edwin R. *Brown America*. New York: Viking Press, 1934.

Fairchild, Henry Pratt. *The Melting-Pot Mistake*. Boston: Little, Brown and Co., 1926.

Frazier, E. Franklin. *Black Bourgeoisie*. New York: Collier, 1962.

_____. *Race and Culture Contacts in the Modern World*. New York: Alfred A. Knopf, 1957.

_____. *The Negro Family in the United States*. Chicago: University of Chicago Press, 1939.

Gavit, John P. *Americans by Choice*. New York: Harper and Brothers, 1922.

Herskovits, Melville J. *The Myth of the Negro Past*. New York: Harper and Brothers, 1941.

Hoffman, Frederick L. *Race Traits and Tendencies of the American Negro*. New York: Macmillan, 1896.

Hughes, Everett C. *Men and Their Work*. Glencoe, Ill.: Free Press, 1958.

Johnson, Charles S. *Growing Up in the Black Belt, Negro Youth in the Rural South*. Washington, D.C.: American Council on Education, 1941.

_____. *Shadow of the Plantation*. Chicago: University of Chicago Press, 1934.

_____ (ed.). *Ebony and Topaz, A Collectanea*. Freeport, N.Y.: Books for Libraries Press, 1971.

Kallen, Horace M. *Individualism: An American Way of Life*. New York: Liveright, 1933.

_____. *Culture and Democracy in the United States: Studies in the Group Psychology of the American Peoples*. New York: Boni and Liveright, 1924.

Klineberg, Otto (ed.). *Characteristics of the American Negro*. New York: Harper and Brothers, 1944.

Lind, Andrew. *An Island Community*. Chicago: University of Chicago Press, 1938.

_____ (ed.). *Race Relations in World Perspective*. Honolulu: University of Hawaii Press, 1955.

Locke, Alain (ed.). *The Negro; An Interpretation.* New York: A. and C. Boni, 1925.
Locke, Alain, and Stern, Bernard (eds.). *When Peoples Meet: A Study in Race and Culture Contacts.* Philadelphia: Progressive Education Association, 1942.
McDougall, William. *Is America Safe for Democracy?* New York: Alfred A. Knopf, 1921.
MacIver, Robert M. (ed.). *Unity and Difference in American Life.* New York: Harper and Brothers, 1947.
_____ (ed.). *Group Relations and Group Antagonisms.* New York: Harper and Brothers, 1944.
Marvick, Elizabeth Wirth, and Reiss, Albert J., Jr. (eds.). *Community Life and Social Policy: Selected Papers by Louis Wirth.* Chicago: University of Chicago Press, 1956.
Masouka, Jitsuichi, and Valien, Preson (eds.). *Race Relations, Problems and Theory, Essays in Honor of Robert E. Park.* Chapel Hill, N.C.: University of North Carolina Press, 1961.
Miller, Herbert A. *Races, Nations and Classes, The Psychology of Domination and Freedom.* Philadelphia: J. P. Lippincott, 1924.
Myrdal, Gunnar, with Richard Sterner and Arnold Rose. *An American Dilemma.* New York: Harper and Brothers, 1944.
Odum, Howard W. and Johnson, Guy B. *The Negro and His Songs.* Chapel Hill, N.C.: University of North Carolina Press, 1925.
Park, Robert E. *The Crowd and the Public and Other Essays*, edited and with an Introduction by Henry Elsner, Jr. Chicago: University of Chicago Press, 1972.
_____. *Race and Culture.* New York: Free Press, 1964.
_____. *Human Communities, The City and Human Ecology.* Glencoe, Ill.: Free Press, 1952.
_____. *The Immigrant Press and Its Control.* New York: Harper and Brothers, 1922.
_____, and Burgess, Ernest W. *Introduction to the Science of Sociology.* Chicago: University of Chicago Press, 1921.
_____; Burgess, E. W.; and McKenzie, Roderick D. *The City.* Chicago: University of Chicago Press, 1925.
Phillips, Ulrich B. *American Negro Slavery.* New York: D. Appleton, 1918.
Powdermaker, Hortense. *After Freedom, A Cultural Study in the Deep South.* New York: Viking Press, 1939.
Reiss, Albert J., Jr. (ed.). *Louis Wirth on Cities and Social Life: Selected Papers.* Chicago: University of Chicago Press, 1964.
Reuter, Ernest B. *Race and Culture Contacts.* New York: McGraw-Hill, 1934.
_____. *Race Mixture, Studies in Intermarriage and Miscegenation.* New York: McGraw-Hill, 1931.

————. *The Mulatto in the United States*. Chicago: University of Chicago Press, 1918.

———— (ed.). *the American Race Problem*. New York: Thomas Y. Crowell Co., 1927.

Rose, Arnold, and Rose, Caroline. *America Divided: Minority Group Relations in the United States*. New York: Alfred A. Knopf, 1953.

Ross, Edward A. *Social Control: A Survey of the Foundations of Order*. New York: Macmillan, 1916.

————. *The Old World in the New: The Significance of Past and Present Immigration to the American People*. New York: The Century Co., 1914.

Shaler, Nathaniel S. *The Neighbor: The Natural History of Human Contacts*. Boston: Houghton, Mifflin and Co., 1904.

Simmel, Ernst (ed.). *Anti-Semitism: A Social Disease*. New York: International Universities Press, 1946.

Stoddard, Lothrop. *The Rising Tide of Color against White World-Supremacy*. New York: Charles Scribner's Sons, 1922.

Stonequist, Everett V. *The Marginal Man*. New York: Charles Scribner's Sons, 1937.

Thomas, William I. *The Unadjusted Girl: With Cases and Standpoint for Behavior Analysis*. Boston: Little, Brown and Co., 1923.

————. *Source Book For Social Origins, Ethnological Materials, Psychological Standpoint, Classified and Annotated Bibliographies for the Interpretation of Savage Society*. Chicago: University of Chicago Press, 1909.

————. *Sex and Society, Studies in the Social Psychology of Sex*. Boston: Richard G. Badger, 1907.

————, and Znaniecki, Florian. *The Polish Peasant in Europe and America*. New York: Alfred A. Knopf, 1927.

————; Park, Robert E.; and Miller, Herbert A. *Old World Traits Transplanted*. New York: Harper and Brothers, 1921.

Thompson, Edgar T. (ed.). *Race Relations and the Race Problem*. Durham, N.C.: Duke University Press, 1939.

————, and Hughes, Everett C. (eds.). *Race, Individual and Collective Behavior*. Glencoe, Ill.: Free Press, 1958.

Tillinghast, Joseph A. *The Negro in Africa and America*. Publications of the American Economic Association. 3 (1902).

Turner, Ralph H. (ed.). *Robert E. Park on Social Control and Collective Behavior*. Chicago: University of Chicago Press, 1967.

Volkart, Edmund H. (ed.) *Social Behavior and Personality, Contributions of W. I. Thomas to Theory and Social Research*. New York: Social Science Research Council, 1951.

Weatherford, Willis D., and Johnson, Charles S. *Race Relations: Adjust-*

ment of Whites and Negroes in the United States. Boston: D. C.
Heath and Co., 1934.
Williams, Robin M., Jr. *The Reduction of Intergroup Tensions: A Survey
of Research on Problems of Ethnic, Racial, and Religious Group
Relations.* New York: Social Science Research Council, 1947.
Wirth, Louis. *The Ghetto.* Chicago: University of Chicago Press, 1928.
Young, Donald. *Research Memorandum on Minority Peoples in the De-
pression.* New York: Social Science Research Council Bulletin 31
(1937).
_____. *American Minority Peoples.* New York: Harper and Brothers,
1932.
_____ (ed.). *The American Negro.* Annals of the American Academy of
Political and Social Science, 140 (1928).

ARTICLES

Abbott, Grace. "True Americanization," *Americanization Bulletin,* 1
(November 1, 1918), 4.
_____. "Democracy of Internationalism; Which We Are Working
Out in Our Immigrant Neighborhoods," *The Survey,* 36 (1916),
478-80.
_____. "The Immigrant as Problem in Community Planning," *American
Journal of Sociology,* 22 (1916), 166-67.
Adamic, Louis. "Thirty Million New Americans," *Harper's Magazine,*
169 (1934), 684-94.
Adams, Romanzo. "The Institute of Pacific Relations," *Journal of
Applied Sociology,* 10 (1925), 63-68.
Addams, Jane. "Nationalism, a Dogma?" *The Survey,* 43 (1920), 524-26.
_____. "Americanization," *Publications of the American Sociological
Society,* 14 (1919), 211-13.
Allport, Floyd. "Culture Conflict Versus the Individual as Factors in
Delinquency," *Social Forces,* 9 (1931), 493-97.
_____. "Group and Institution as Concept in a Natural Science of Social
Phenomena," *Publications of the American Sociological Society,*
22 (1928), 83-99.
_____. "The Group Fallacy in Relation to Social Science," *American
Journal of Sociology,* 19 (1924), 688-706.
Bain, Read. "Cultural Integration and Social Conflict," *American Journal
of Sociology,* 44 (1939), 499-509.
Bernard, Luther L. "The Significance of Environment as a Social Factor,"
Publications of the American Sociological Society, 16 (1922), 84-112.
Bernard, William S. "Cultural Determinants of Naturalization," *Ameri-
can Sociological Review,* 1 (1936), 943-53.

Berry, J. Brewton. "The Concept of Race in Sociology Textbooks," *Social Forces*, 18 (1940), 411-17.

Blumer, Herbert. "Race Prejudice as a Sense of Group Position," *Pacific Sociological Review*, 1 (1958), 3-7.

Boas, Franz. "The Question of Racial Purity," *American Mercury*, 3 (1924), 163-69.

Bogardus, Emory S. "Racial Enclavement," *Sociology and Social Research*, 25 (1940-41), 460-65.

_____. "The Personality Clash and Social Distance," *Journal of Applied Sociology*, 11 (1926), 166-74.

Bond, Horace M. "Negro Leadership Since Washington," *South Atlantic Quarterly*, 24 (1925), 115-30.

_____. "What the Army 'Intelligence' Tests Measured," *Opportunity*, 2 (1924), 197-202.

Bourne, Randolph. "Trans-National America," *The Atlantic Monthly*, 118 (1916), 86-97.

Brown, Francis J. "Sociology and Intercultural Understanding," *Journal of Educational Sociology*, 12 (1938-39), 328-31.

Brown, Sterling. "Negro Characters as Seen by White Authors," *Journal of Negro Education*, 2 (1933), 180.

Brown, W. O. "The Nature of Race Consciousness," *Social Forces*, 10 (1931), 90-97.

Bunche, Ralph J. "The Programs of Organizations Devoted to the Improvement of the Status of the Negro," *Journal of Negro Education*, 8 (1939), 539-50.

_____. "A Critical Analysis of the Tactics and Programs of Minority Groups," *Journal of Negro Education*, 4 (1935), 308-20.

Burden, Romare. "The Negro Artist and Modern Art," *Opportunity*, 12 (1934), 12.

Cash, Wilbur J. "The Mind of the South," *American Mercury*, 18 (1929), 185-92.

Cayton, Horace. "The Psychological Approach to Race Relations," *Reed College Bulletin*, 25 (1946), 8-27.

_____. "Negro Morale," *Opportunity*, 19 (1941), 371-75.

_____. "Negroes Live in Chicago," *Opportunity*, 15 (1937), 366-69, and 16 (1938), 12-14.

Cole, Stewart G. "Cultural Democracy in War and Peace," *Journal of Educational Sociology*, 16 (1942-43), 332-34.

Coser, Lewis A. "Europe's Neurotic Nationalism: Tribalism Replaces Freedom and the Rights of Men," *Commentary*, 1 (1946), 58-63.

Davie, Maurice R. "Minorities: A Challenge to American Democracy," *Journal of Educational Sociology*, 12 (1938-39), 451-56.

Davis, Allison. "Our Negro 'Intellectuals,' " *The Crisis*, 35 (1928), 268-69, 284-86.

Day, Caroline Bond. "Race-Crossings in the United States," *The Crisis*, 37 (1930), 81-82, 103.

Du Bois, W.E.B. "Criteria of Negro Art," *The Crisis*, 32 (1926), 296.

"East By West: Our Windows on the Pacific, *The Survey Graphic*, Number 56 (1926), 133-96.

Fischer, Rudolph. "The Caucasian Storms Harlem," *American Mercury*, 8 (1926), 393-98.

Francis, E. K. "The Nature of the Ethnic Group," *American Journal of Sociology*, 52 (1946-47), 393-400.

Frazier, E. Franklin. "Race Contacts and the Social Structure," *American Sociological Review*, 14 (1949), 1-11.

_____. "Human, All too Human, the Negro's Vested Interest in Segregation," *Survey Graphic*, 36 (1947), 74-75, 99-100.

_____. "Sociological Theory and Race Relations," *American Sociological Review*, 12 (1947), 265-71.

_____. "Ethnic and Minority Groups in Wartime with Special Reference to the Negro," *American Journal of Sociology*, 48 (1942), 369-77.

_____. "Negro Harlem: An Ecological Study," *American Journal of Sociology*, 43 (1937), 72-88.

_____. "The Du Bois Program in the Present Crisis," *Race*, 1 (1935-36), 11-13.

_____. "Folk Culture in the Making," *Southern Workingman*, 57 (1927), 195-99.

_____. "The Pathology of Race Prejudice," *Forum*, 70 (1927), 856-62.

_____. "Garvey: A Mass Leader," *The Nation*, 128 (1926), 147-48.

_____. "The Garvey Movement," *Opportunity*, 4 (1926), 346-48.

Glazer, Nathan. "Integration of American Immigrants," *Law and Contemporary Problems*, 21 (1956), 256-69.

Gordon, Eugene. "The Negro's Inhibitions," *American Mercury*, 13 (1928), 159-65.

Handlin, Oscar. "Group Life Within the American Pattern: Its Scope and its Limits," *Commentary*, 8 (1949), 411-17.

Hansen, Marcus L. "The Third Generation in America," *Commentary*, 14 (1952), 492-500.

Herskovits, Melville. "A Critical Discussion of the Mulatto Hypothesis," *Journal of Negro Education*, 3 (1934), 389-402.

Holsey, Alban L. "Learning How to Be Black," *American Mercury*, 16 (1929), 421-25.

Hughes, Langston. "The Negro Artist and the Racial Mountain," *The Nation*, 122 (1926), 692-94.

Hussey, L. M. "Afra-american, North and South," *American Mercury*, 6 (1925), 196-200.

———. "Homo Africanus," *American Mercury*, 4 (1925), 83-89.

Jencks, Albert Ernest. "Assimilation in the Philippines as Interpreted in Terms of Assimilation in America," *American Journal of Sociology*, 19 (1913-14), 773-91.

Johnson, Charles S. "Robert E. Park: In Memoriam," *Sociology and Social Research*, 28 (1944), 354-58.

———. "The Present Status and Trends of the Negro Family," *Social Forces*, 16 (1937), 247-57.

———. "The Rise of the Negro Magazine," *Journal of Negro History*, 13 (1928), 7-21.

———. "The Social Philosophy of Booker T. Washington," *Opportunity*, 6 (1928), 102-5, 115.

———. "The New Frontage on American Life," in Alain Locke (ed.), *The New Negro: An Interpretation*. New York: A. and C. Boni, 1925.

———. Editorials in *Opportunity*, 2 (1924), 3-4, 194.

Johnson, James Weldon. "The Dilemma of the Negro Author," *American Mercury*, 15 (1928), 477-81.

Kallen, Horace M. "Democracy versus the Melting Pot: A Study of American Nationality," *The Nation*, 100 (1915), 190-94, 217-20.

———. "Zionism and the Struggle Toward Democracy," *The Nation*, 101 (1915), 379-80.

Kennedy, Ruby Jo Reeves. "Single or Triple Melting Pot? Inter-marriage Trends in New Haven, 1870-1940," *American Journal of Sociology*, 49 (1943-44), 331-39.

Landecker, Werner. "Functional Analysis of Intergroup Relations," *Sociology and Social Research*, 25 (1940-41), 431-40.

Lasker, Bruno. "The Negro in Detroit," *The Survey*, 15 (1926), 72-73, 123.

Lewin, Kurt. "Self-Hatred Among Jews," *Contemporary Jewish Record*, 4 (1941), 219-32.

Locke, Alain. "Of Native Sons: Real and Otherwise," *Opportunity*, 19 (1941), 48.

———. "Dry Fields and Green Pastures," *Opportunity*, 18 (1940), 41.

———. "The Negro: 'New' or Newer," *Opportunity*, 17 (1939), 36.

———. "Jingo, Counter-Jingo and Us," *Opportunity*, 16 (1938), 7, 39.

———. "God Save Reality!" *Opportunity*, 15 (1937), 8, 40.

———. "Deep River: Deeper Sea," *Opportunity*, 14 (1936), 6, 42.

———. "Harlem: Dark Weather-Vane," *Survey Graphic*, 25 (1936), 456-58.

———. "The Eleventh Hour of Nordicism," *Opportunity*, 13 (1935), 46.

_____. "The Saving Grace of Realism," *Opportunity*, 12 (1934), 8-9.

_____. "Black Truth and Black Beauty," *Opportunity*, 11 (1933), 14.

_____. "1928: A Retrospective Review," *Opportunity*, 7 (1929), 8.

_____. "Beauty Instead of Ashes," *The Nation*, 126 (1928), 432-44.

_____. "American Literary Tradition and the Negro," *Modern Quarterly*, 3 (1926), 215-22.

_____. "A Note on African Art," *Opportunity*, 2 (1924), 134-38.

McKenzie, Roderick D. "The Oriental Invasion," *Journal of Applied Sociology*, 10 (1925), 120-30.

McLean, Helen. "Race Prejudice," *American Journal of Orthopsychiatry*, 14 (1944), 705-13.

Matthews, Brander. "The Rise and Fall of Negro Minstrelsy," *Scribner's Magazine*, 57 (1915), 754.

Miller, Herbert A. "Some Universals in the Race Problem," *Opportunity*, 3 (1925), 6-7.

_____. "Science, Pseudo-Science and the Race Question," *The Crisis*, 30 (1925), 287.

_____. "Patriotism and Internationalism," *Proceedings of the American Sociological Society*, 16 (1922), 135.

_____. "The Complexity of the Americanization Problem," *Pacific Review*, I (1920), 132-38.

_____. "Nationalism in Bohemia and Poland," *North American Review*, 200 (1914), 879-86.

_____. "The Rising National Individualism," *Proceedings of the American Sociological Society*, 8 (1914), 49-61.

Miller, Kelly. "Is Race Prejudice Innate or Acquired?," *Journal of Applied Sociology*, 11 (1927), 516-24.

Park, Robert E. "Life History," *American Journal of Sociology*, 79 (1973), 251-60.

_____. "Method of Teaching: Impressions and a Verdict," *Social Forces*, 10 (1941), 36-53.

_____. "The Concept of Social Distance," *Journal of Applied Sociology*, 8 (1924), 329-34.

_____. "In a Black Belt Town," *Southern Workman*, 42 (1913), 142-51.

Reuter, Ernest B. "Racial Theory," *American Journal of Sociology*, 50 (1945), 452-61.

_____. "Why the Presence of the Negro Constitutes a Problem in the American Social Order," *Journal of Negro Education*, 8 (1939), 291-98.

_____. "The Relation of Biology and Sociology," *American Journal of Sociology*, 32 (1927), 705-18.

_____. "Sociology and Biology," *Publications of the American Sociological Society*, 19 (1925), 56-67.

_____. "Immigration and the American Birth Rate," *Journal of Applied Sociology*, 8 (1924), 274-78.

Roucek, Joseph S. "The Problem of Becoming Americanized," *Sociology and Social Research*, 17 (1932-33), 243-50.

_____, and Brown, Francis J. "The Problem of the Negro and European Immigrant Minorities: Some Comparisons and Contrasts,"*Journal of Negro Education*, 8 (1939), 299-312.

Shuyler, George. "A Negro Looks Ahead," *American Mercury*, 19 (1930), 212-20.

_____. "Our White Folks," *American Mercury*, 12 (1927), 385-92.

_____. "The Negro Art Hokum," *The Nation*, 122 (1926), 662-63.

Standing, T. G. "Nationalism in Negro Leadership," *American Journal ' of Sociology*, 40 (1934), 180-92.

Thomas, William I. "The Prussian-Polish Situation; An Experiment in Assimilation," *American Journal of Sociology*, 19 (1914), 624-29.

_____. "Race Psychology: Standpoint and Questionnaire, with Particular Reference to the Immigrant and the Negro," *American Journal of Sociology*, 17 (1912), 725-75.

_____. "Eugenics: The Science of Breeding Men," *American Magazine*, 68 (1909), 190-97.

_____. "The Significance of the Orient for the Occident," *Publications of the American Sociological Society*, 2 (1907), 111-23.

_____. "The Psychology of Race-Prejudice," *American Journal of Sociology*, 9 (1904), 593-611.

Thurman, Wallace. "Negro Artists and the Negro," *The New Republic*, 52 (1927), 37-39.

_____. "Nephews of Uncle Remus," *The Independent*, 119 (1927), 296-98.

Walling, W. E. "Race War in the North," *The Independent*, 65 (1908), 530.

Weatherly, U. G. "Social Pluralism," *Sociology and Social Research*, 18 (1933-34), 103-9.

_____. "The Racial Element in Social Assimilation," *American Journal of Sociology*, 16 (1911), 593-611.

_____. "Race and Marriage," *American Journal of Sociology*, 15 (1909), 433-53.

Wirth, Louis. "Research in Racial and Cultural Relations," *Midwest Journal*, 1 (1948-50), 14-23.

_____. "Group Tensions and Mass Democracy," *American Scholar*, 14 (1945), 231.

_____. "Morale and Minority Groups," *American Journal of Sociology*, 47 (1941), 415-33.

_____. "Culture Conflict and Misconduct," *Social Forces*, 9 (1931), 484-92.

INDEX

About the Author

R. FRED WACKER is Assistant Professor in the Social Science Division of Wayne State University's Weekend College in Detroit. His articles have appeared in the journals *Ethnic Groups* and *Phylon*.